# THE ACADEMIC LIBRARY IN TIMES OF RETRENCHMENT

Proceedings of a conference
of the
Library and Information Research Group
16-18 July 1982

edited by
## Colin Harris and Lesley Gilder

## rossendale

© Rossendale 1983
  500 Chesham House,
  150 Regent Street,
  LONDON W1R 5FA


ISBN O 946138 O2 8


British Library Cataloguing in Publication Data
_____

The Academic library in times of retrenchment.
  1. Library, University and college
  2. Library finance
  I. Harris, Colin    II. Gilder, Lesley
  025.1'977    2675.U5

  ISBN 0-946138-02-8

# CONTENTS

# FOREWORD

*The Academic Library in Times of Retrenchment* was a
residential conference of the Library and Information
Research Group, and was attended by a substantial number
of delegates from a wide range of libraries and library
schools. Those presenting papers spoke from immediate
experience and with authority, outlining the implications
of national developments, both political and technological,
for academic libraries. They pointed towards permanent
change in our apprehension of the role and function of the
academic library, both within its own institutional environment and in a wider context. The implications for the library
manager in terms of policy formulation, planning, decision
making, staffing and services were presented with clarity.
All of the speakers had been involved with research in the
library and information field, either as researchers themselves or as advisors and administrators.

The majority of papers dealt with the problems and
opportunities of retrenchment from an operational stand-
pont. Data and statistics, in-house research, new technology,
co-operation and the library manager's response were examined
in detail, following Norman Higham's comprehensive introduction
to the theme of the seminar. In this he instanced significant
professional activities since the Robbins report of 1963,
leading up to the recent reports of the Library and Information
Services Council, and an increased parliamentary interest. He
saw the predominant strategy as that of survival, necessitating
a political approach and greater co-ordination. Indeed, the
recurring theme of the need for increased political awareness
and mastery combined with a sound grasp of grass roots
developments characterised much of the lengthy formal and
informal discussions which took place at the conference.
Research was seen as an indispensable aid in achieving this
aim. It remains to be seen whether developments in practice
will reflect a determination to act in the same positive spirit.

# THE ACADEMIC LIBRARY IN TIMES OF RETRENCHMENT : THE NATIONAL SCENE

Norman Higham
*Librarian, University of Bristol*

One has to start somewhere; I start with the Robbins Report (1) of 1963 and the expansion of higher education. The new universities were already either formed or about to be so; the colleges of advanced technology were on the point of becoming universities of technology and a number of colleges were about to merge and become polytechnics. And all were to expand, to provide an advanced education for all young people capable of benefitting from it. The government of the day saw progress and well-being in the expansion of higher education within a white-hot technological revolution. They were stirring times, though some of us in libraries wondered about an expansion that increased by so many the number of institutions and therefore the number of libraries, all having to build up bread-and-butter collections before they could spread the jam on them. And we wondered how thinly the jam would have eventually to be spread. Why not, we said, expand existing institutions?  We had not really read Robbins or the government's mind carefully enough. The existing institutions just could not have coped. But all those new institutions needed large amounts of recurrent money for books and periodicals, and capital for buildings. And how!

The needs of libraries in higher education were recognised in the formation by the University Grants Committee of the Committee on Libraries, the Parry Committee. Its Report (2), described once as the most ignored major national report, was read enthusiastically only by university librarians, for it said so much of what we wanted to hear. If Robbins was the battle cry, Parry was the laurel wreath. Libraries were the central organs of their institutions, and it was we who played on them!  They needed more money to keep them in tune;

some of them got it, some did not. But it was a time when we appeared to be building for the future.

If the Government did not read the report closely enough to give us the promised land, it did note its recommendation that:

> 'The library departments of the British Museum should become the British National Library and as many as possible of the functions listed below should be carried out by that Institution as a matter of urgency. The finance necessary to carry out these services, which we judge to be of prime importance for the proper development of library and information services for universities and for the country as a whole, should be made available to the British Museum as soon as possible.' (3)

It went on to list interlending, union catalogue maintenance, central national provision, coverage of foreign material, bibliographic services, library research, training, copyright holding and co-ordination of library services.

Within a year Edward Short, the then Secretary of State for Education, set up the National Libraries Committee under the chairmanship of Dr. (now Sir Frederick) Dainton to examine the various national libraries, and to consider whether they should be brought into a unified framework. The main recommendation of the Dainton Committee in June 1969 (4) was the creation of a National Libraries Authority. Within two years Command Paper 4572 (5) announced the Government's intention to create the British Library, and by 1973 it was born.

At the same time as a dream was realised and a mammoth national library organisation had come into existence, a new economic situation was imposing itself on the educational institutions which stood to gain most from a strong national library system. Inflation was rising and the beginning of a freeze was setting in. The 1974/5 Annual Report of my University's Council to Court sounded the first warning for many years:

> 'It became clear early in 1973 that the year 1974/5, the third in the present quinquennium, would be a particularly difficult one. The customary supplementation for rising prices was wholly denied to us, and this at a time when inflation in university items of expenditure was running at 20%, and the April budget dealt further severe blows.' (6)

I lost ten percent of my library staff by the freezing of
vacancies, and only part of that number was restored in
subsequent years. One has to be reminded, in the troubles
of 1981/82, that 1974/75 was a critical year, and it set
the tone for what was to come.

After the expansion of Robbins, the consolidation of
Parry, the nationalisation of Dainton, came contraction,
financial but also physical.

> 'By the end of 1974', said Sir Frederick Dainton (in
> April 1976 by now Chairman of the UGC), 'the University
> Grants Committee had come to the conclusion that they
> were clearly not going to have enough resources, either
> in the short term or the long term, to build new
> libraries at all universities on the scale needed to
> match an indefinitely growing number of books. Even if
> this had been possible it was doubtful whether it would
> have been the most sensible course to follow.' (7)

He said this in the foreword of the report of the UGC working
party which had been set up in 1975 to consider capital
provision for university libraries, under the chairmanship
of Professor Richard Atkinson. The Atkinson Report and the
concept of the self-renewing library are well enough known
to need no further explanation.

In March 1977 the Library Management Research Unit at
Loughborough (now CLAIM) set up a seminar to identify the
issues which needed to be investigated following the Atkinson
Report and the discussion that arose from it. In a paper
setting out SCONUL's view I said:

> 'The paucity of information on which the main recommenda-
> tions of the Atkinson Report were based was an outcome
> of the shortage of time available. The paucity of
> information on which the criticism was based was an
> outcome of the discrete nature of the information (if
> indeed it can be so called). Decision-making in an
> uncertain environment is what most of us do most of the
> time, and the use of libraries is such a personal matter
> that its study is correspondingly complex. Libraries have
> been ill-equipped to carry out such investigations but
> if we are to test our beliefs in order to plan for the
> future a way must be found.

In general terms then we need more research into the use of libraries. The work that has already been done in this field has had to be based largely on easily obtainable data. The problem in dealing with the research use by an individual scholar in a library is to obtain useful data without distortion. But if we are to defend, as SCONUL sets out to do, the retention of large quantities of little-used material in our libraries, then we must find ways of gathering evidence that will establish the need beyond doubt. And if we find that impossible we shall be in the position of having to defend a belief without supporting hard evidence. This is neither uncommon nor disreputable - 'I know that my Redeemer liveth' is a respectable precedent - but we may not command respect.' (8)

Early in 1977 the UGC set up its own Steering Group on Library Research, following the recommendation in the Atkinson Report that the effects of applying its recommendations should be monitored. The Steering Group was charged with the task of defining and recommending (i) what information should be requested from universities about library operations, and (ii) any specific research projects needed to make possible a reliable evaluation of any library operation which may affect financial provision for libraries, and of the principle of the self-renewing library. The Steering Group looked at research projects sponsored by the British Library Research and Development Department (BLRDD) and saw as high priority areas, library statistics, capital and recurrent costs, relegation to reserve storage, and the effectiveness of libraries. Other matters for investigation were to be the scope for specialisation, methods and costs of disposal, and the problems of special collections. Since that time the Group has collected very detailed statistics from university libraries and carried out analyses. These have been a help in establishing needs for accommodation in individual cases. At an early stage the Group asked Geoffrey Ford, then of the Centre for Research on User Studies, to study current practice in stock relegation in university libraries. A shortened version of the report of this work was published in the *Journal of Librarianship* for January 1980 (9). A literature review by CLAIM was also commissioned by the Steering Group, and was published in 1981 by CLAIM as No. 3 of their report series (10). The Group set up a 'cost options working party' in 1978 to compare the costs of building and servicing additional local storage with the disposal of least-used material and using interloan to retrieve when necessary. It found that it is cheaper to discard when the prospective frequency of demand falls below once in thirteen years. The use of cheaper purpose-built reserve storage would move the break-even point to once every twenty years. It was noted that only costs were being considered, and the effect of delays on the user and any distortion due to in-library use (ignored in the project) were matters for further investigation. An article based on the Working Party's tentative findings was published by Professor A.J. Brown in the *Journal of Librarianship* for October 1980 (11).

A pilot study of the coverage by certain libraries of items found in a number of Ph.D. theses was undertaken as an attempt to investigate library effectiveness. It is hoped to extend this study, and Peter Stone and Geoffrey Ford have carried out work on the use of books in the Universities of Sussex and Southampton. Discussions were held with the Universities of Leicester, Loughborough and Nottingham to investigate the possibilities of more effective use of resources by local inter-library collaboration. It found the results interesting but could not recommend the allocation of scarce funds to support further developments. The Group took up the problem of conservation in its discussions and invited Mr. Nicholas Barker, Head of Conservation, British Library, to present a paper. This graphically showed the extent of the problem nationally, and the Group agreed to keep under review work being carried out in the British Library and elsewhere.

I have gone into some detail on the UGC Steering Group because little is known about its work, and I hope I have made clear that it is a body at a national level through which research on academic library problems could be channelled and which may be able to support investigations. Since the UGC is also the body which is imposing cuts on behalf of the Government on universities, it is therefore itself very short of funds, and the work of the Steering Group has been hampered by shortage of secretarial support.

Meanwhile, other national developments of a wider nature were taking place. Back in 1974, after Parry and Dainton and the formation of the BL, SCONUL began discussions on the idea of a national co-ordinating body for libraries. Parry had recommended, not only the formation of what is called the British National Library, but also a British Library Services Council linking advisory committees for national libraries,

Library Advisory Councils for England and Wales and a UGC Sub-Committee for Libraries (recommended elsewhere in its report - we got the Steering Group instead). The BLSC would report to the Secretary of State for Education and Science. SCONUL's discussions did not get very far at that stage; the consensus of opinion was that, so soon after the British Library's formation, we should wait to see if it performed its role as the hub of the country's library system before proposing another body. A working party was set up, however, and identified four main areas where there appeared to be a need to formulate a national policy; co-ordination of library and information resources, co-ordination of technical services, co-ordination of technical and bibliographical standards, and the preservation of national library resources. It saw that there was no overall body that could speak for the UK to UNESCO, IFLA, etc. on these matters. A report along these lines was produced in January 1976, which did not excite attention. A golden opportunity came to give it an airing in the corridors of power, however, when SCONUL was invited to submit oral evidence to the Education, Arts and Home Office Sub-Committee of the Expenditure Committee of the House of Commons in May 1978. This was quite by chance, since I was on the delegation from the Library Association which gave oral evidence, and, because I was Chairman of SCONUL at the time, I was asked if I would like to return with a delegation from SCONUL.  During that session we were able to draw attention to our views on the need for a national co-ordinating body and were invited to submit our report. The Expenditure Committee's report in June 1978 contained the following paragraph:

> 'The report of the SCONUL Working Party on the need for a national co-ordinating body on library policy of January 1976 expresses disquiet at the proliferation of bodies concerned with or responsible for library policy and the lack of any 'formal machinery for consultation and co-ordination on a national scale'. We share this disquiet, and *recommend that the DES should set up a Committee to examine as a matter of urgency the whole relationship between the Department, national, public, university, and other libraries and library advisory councils.*' (12)

Though the Library Association's memorandum of February 1978 was not specifically mentioned, no doubt its recommendations along similar lines also had some effect. The Association's specific recommendation that the Library Advisers should be given greater status and influence was wholly supported by the Expenditure Committee.

We were not surprised when the Office of Arts and Libraries (OAL) replied to the Expenditure Committee's recommendation along the lines that they had already set up a committee. Certainly the Library Advisory Council for England - LAC(E) - had shortly before set up a Working Party and it bore some resemblance to what the Select Committee was looking for; we were not surprised, because the officers of OAL were closely in touch with both the library world and government and saw the way the wind was blowing. That working party produced a report which was submitted to the then Minister for the Arts in May 1979, and which formed the first part of what has now been published (in April 1982) as *The Future Development of Libraries and Information Services* (13). Part I is called the Organisational and Policy Framework and is known to the *cognoscenti* as FD1.

After various recommendations about the responsibilities of DES and an exhortation that it should take an active part in discussions and consultations with the educational, scientific and library worlds, the report turned to the Library Advisory Council itself. It recommended extending the membership to provide a broader representation 'of interests and experience in all kinds of library including senior administrators as well as practising professionals, authority members and library users' (14). It also recommended that the Council should 'undertake the intensive and continuing analysis of policy issues, providing it with a sufficient allocation of funds to support research and consultancies, and call for an annual report to the Secretary of State on its activities which could be incorporated in the Department's annual report to Parliament' (15). The Working Party noted that the LAC had already 'embarked upon a comprehensive study of the needs and other pressures which would influence the future development of the country's library services...' (16). This study was intended to cover (i) the changing objectives of libraries of different kinds and the interaction between them, (ii) the likely impact of technological development, (iii) the need to make accessible an increasing wealth of books and information, (iv) constraints on public expenditure, forcing a more cost-effective approach, and (v) the present lack of machinery for national planning and co-ordination. The Working Party emphasised that FD1 dealt only with the last matter and commented that their studies had underlined the need for the Council to pursue the remaining matters as soon as possible. It also made the point that it was beyond its scope to carry out the enquiry recommended by the Expenditure Committee because that was intended to cover the U.K. as a whole and LAC(E) was not so empowered. However it was clear that FDI was looking in the direction of a national co-ordinating body. And it was clear that the Working Party saw LAC(E) as potentially capable of being that body. Back in 1974 SCONUL had considered LAC(E) as a possible contender for the job of national co-ordination, but had rejected it for two main reasons. One was that it covered only England as noted above; the other was what it saw as the 'track record' of LAC(E), which had not in the past encouraged the view that it could encompass the whole library scene outside public libraries and lead a movement to gain government support for greater co-ordination of services.

The Minister's reply in August 1980 conceded little, but OAL and the Library Advisory Council showed signs of enthusiasm at the idea of LAC(E) as a national co-ordinating body with a new interesting role and a new lease of life. In January 1980 it had set up its second Working Party 'to consider the objectives of libraries and information services of all kinds, and the scope for enhancing and supporting the library and information network and for making better use of available resources. This scope was to include the application of new technology, and improved forms of co-operation at local, regional and national levels' (17). Its report under the title *Working together within a national framework,* formed the second part (FD2) of the main report referred to earlier *(The future development of libraries and information services).* Changes had taken place in the Council and OAL in the period between the setting up of the Working Party and the publication of its report, and they were significant. The Council was renamed the Library and Information Services Council (LISC) and a professional librarian and library educator, Professor Wilfred Saunders, had been appointed as its Chairman. John Gray, previously Head of BLRDD, was appointed Adviser on information matters to the Minister.

The Working Party was also able to refer to another parliamentary initiative in the information field. At the beginning of 1980 the Education, Science and Arts Committee of the House of Commons (the Price Committee) decided, after discussion with the Minister for the Arts, to consider information storage and retrieval 'not only in the library field but also in that of science and technology' (18). Once again representatives of the Library Association (this time with a representative of the Institute of Information Scientists) and of SCONUL gave oral evidence as did those of the British Library, OAL and Aslib. The report *Information storage and retrieval in the British library service* (19) (and this means the library service of Britain) made six recommendations:

(1)  The problem of the implications for copyright of new technology should be treated urgently.

(2)  The second report of LISC (FD2) should be published as soon as possible to assist the achievement of a national library policy.

(3)  The relationship between the co-operative library groups and the British Library should be given renewed attention.

(4)  An automated information network system should be developed and co-ordinated on a national basis.

(5)  The Government should appoint a Minister of Cabinet rank to be responsible for information policy.

(6)  A Standing Commission should be set up as a matter of urgency, widely representative of interests concerned with the provision of information 'particularly by telematic means', to examine the problems of developing a national information network.

The LISC Working Party considered these recommendations in the course of its investigations. It noted that the Government had decided that the Minister for the Arts should undertake the ministerial responsibilities referred to above, assisted by LISC. It recommended that LISC should undertake the responsibilities for which some had wanted a Standing Commission. It recommended a review of centres of excellence. It recommended formal arrangements for keeping under review the progress and application of new technology. (A Working Group on electronic publishing has now been established under the chairmanship of Julain Blackwell with instructions to report to the Minister urgently). It recommended that developments in co-operation should take place 'within the framework now emerging for the co-ordination of national policy' (20). It said that some expenditure on setting-up and pump-priming in the field of co-operation will be necessary, and it is at present lacking. It recommended a review of future financing of library and information services within a national co-ordinating framework, and particularly the financing of the publication and dissemination of new information - a problem highlighted by a report of the Royal Society in 1981 (21). It also recommended that a review of future manpower and training requirements should be the subject of the Council's next major report. A Working Party has already been set up by LISC on this subject and is hard at work.

Meanwhile, independently of the Office of Arts and Libraries, a study had been commissioned by the Advisory Council for Applied Research and Development (ACARD) 'to consider whether the development and application of information technology in the UK should be stimulated' (22). It was clear that this study was industry-related and it is not surprising that a main recommendation in its report resulted in the appointment by the Government of a Minister for Information Technology within the Department of Industry and Trade.

Meanwhile, back at the OAL, the Minister for the Arts had delivered the closing address at the Annual Conference of the Library Association in September 1981 at Cliftonville. It contained a lot of ministerial language, it flattered and cajoled, and it has been regarded by some as merely bland. With some awareness of the background against which it was produced I believe that it was an important speech, and marked a turning point (symbolically, if you like) in official, even government, attitudes to the library and information community. There were some important pointers among the Minister's words to opportunities for making our views known and influencing decisions. I believe that what has been brought about during the period I have been summarising, brought about at times painfully slowly, at times by chance and surprisingly quickly, is an atmosphere in which we can help significantly in effecting changes, not merely in our own organisations and institutions, but in the social and economic development of the country as a whole.

I do not intend to end on this optimistic, not to say starry-eyed note. There appears to be a climate of opinion at a national level which is encouraging for the development of library and information services. But it has come at a time of critical economic difficulty. To talk of pump-priming and development funds today appears totally unrealistic. Most of us are suffering larger real cuts in our grants than ever before. Universities are talking of survival rather than of development and our libraries are vulnerable. My university talks of protecting the library when it means protecting the funds for purchasing books and periodicals, while inadequate library staff numbers are to be cut by over 15%. The UGC is seen as having become the instrument of Treasury surgery rather than a 'bridge and bulwark' between autonomous universities and the Government. Polytechnics, looking with some anxiety at the 'Trojan horse of a National body' (23), are cutting library budgets, and smaller higher education colleges are facing closure over the next few years. Have they brought us our 'bow of burning gold' when we are too weak to pull back the string?  As librarians we are eager to make our not inconsiderable resources available under appropriate conditions to the whole community. This has not been easy in the past, but now we are struggling to make our resources available even to our own staff and students.

The country needs the co-ordination of library and information services to achieve the most effective exploitation of a vast resource, not at present effectively, cost-effectively, used. But co-ordination must work to the benefit of all services, and all services include *our* services. We are not in a position to give any more except some expertise, goodwill and a co-operative spirit. These, however, may be very significant, because we still know too little and have much to find out to be sure that we are using resources in the most efficient way. I spoke of decision-making in an uncertain environment, and we certainly do that; but we must reduce the areas of uncertainty though we shall never eliminate them. All of us try to do this in our own libraries to some extent. We rarely call it research, since it is a necessary part of good management, but it involves investigation however quick and dirty. In proposing how cuts were to be applied at Bristol my Vice-Chancellor said in his paper to Senate that though whenever he went

into the Library he was impressed by the amount of trivia
and ephemera we acquire, he was nevertheless seized of the
importance of building up and maintaining collections of
excellence. If it was a matter of choosing between
cutting collections and cutting services he believed
there was only one answer. (24)

This at least expressed a positive attitude, shared by
many; and at a time of survival I also would stress the
supremacy of acquisition. But who knows the effect on a
university's educational programme of neglecting *either*
acquisitions or services? And what services? On-line information retrieval services have been a godsend to some
researchers. What is their cost-effectiveness? How many books,
or periodicals or how many staff are they worth? And if we
know, who will believe us? Will academic decision-makers, who
have more information than they can cope with, and too much
administration to have time to use any of it? If we are in a
survival situation, what should survive? What do we do about
opening hours, lending services, interloans, readers' assistance?
Is 'user education' important enough now to use up reduced
staff resources? We can all answer these questions, but how
far are our answers based on information and how far on
prejudice or belief? 'I know that my Redeemer liveth' - yes,
but show us your methodology.

Some investigations can still be done in our own libraries,
or can be if we have enough staff left. Other investigations,
which will help us in our libraries and help us to survive
cuts are best done nationally. We have OAL, LISC, BL, Aslib,
CRUS, CLAIM, the UGC Steering Group and the Department of
Trade and Industry (especially in Information Technology Year)
all interested in research at a national level. We must take
advantage of whatever opportunities this line-up presents.
You will be identifying themes in more detail at this
conference. And, in addition, there are possible developments
which cannot get off the ground for lack of development, not
research, funds. This is where national co-ordination must
come in. We have done something, some have done a great deal,
individually and in small groups, often with support from the
British Library and other organisations. We should now be
thinking, not merely in terms of national support for our
own ideas and projects, but thinking nationally, not merely
nationally in terms of libraries but nationally in terms of
educational institutions and of their contribution to society.

If we do that and act accordingly we shall, as a by-product,
enhance the status of the library and information community
in the country. The Minister for the Arts in his address
chided us for not speaking effectively enough. We must
identify the problems, some old, some new and very difficult,
knock on the Minister's door and get colleagues in LISC to
knock on the council table and demand that we be given
adequate support, financial and organisational, to solve
them. We are more likely to be listened to now than ever
before.

REFERENCES

1.  COMMITTEE ON HIGHER EDUCATION. *Higher education; report
    of the Committee appointed by the Prime Minister under
    the chairmanship of Lord Robbins 1961-1963.* London:
    HMSO, 1963 (Cmnd. 2154).

2.  UNIVERSITY GRANTS COMMITTEE. *Report of the Committee
    on Libraries.* London: HMSO, 1967.

3.  *ibid.* para 635(a), p.160.

4.  DEPARTMENT OF EDUCATION AND SCIENCE. *Report of the
    National Libraries Committee.* London: HMSO, 1969
    (Cmnd. 4028).

5.  The British Library. 1971. Cmnd. 4572.

6.  UNIVERSITY OF BRISTOL. Report of Council to Court and
    statements of accounts, 1974-75, Bristol, 1975. p.1.

7.  DAINTON, F. Foreword to UNIVERSITY GRANTS COMMITTEE.
    *Capital provision for university libraries.* London:
    HMSO, 1976.

8.  HIGHAM, N. SCONUL's broad view. *In:* Blackwood, J.W. *(ed).
    The future of library collections: proceedings of a
    seminar held by the Library Management Research Unit,
    University of Technology, Loughborough, 21-23 March 1977.*
    Loughborough: Library Management Research Unit, 1977
    (LMRU Report No. 7), pp.14-15.

9.  FORD, G. Stock relegation in some British university
    libraries. *Journal of Librarianship,* 12 (1), January 1980,
    42-55.

10. GILDER, L. *et al. The relegation and storage of material in academic libraries: a literature review.* Loughborough: Centre for Library and Information Management, 1980 (CLAIM Report No.3).

11. BROWN, A.J. Some library costs and options. *Journal of Librarianship,* 12(4), October 1980, 211-216.

12. EIGHTH REPORT FROM THE EXPENDITURE COMMITTEE SESSION 1977-78. Select public expenditure programmes ch.4 provision for museum galleries, and libraries H.C. 600-iv, 361-i, ii and iii, 1977-

13. DEPARTMENT OF EDUCATION AND SCIENCE OFFICE OF ARTS AND LIBRARIES. *The future development of libraries and information services.* London: HMSO, 1982, (Library Information Series No.12).

14. *ibid.* Part 1, para.59(1).

15. *ibid.* Part 1, para.59(5).

16. *ibid.* Part 1, para.60.

17. *ibid.* Part 2, para.1.

18. EDUCATION, SCIENCE AND ARTS COMMITTEE (HOUSE OF COMMONS). *Information storage and retrieval in the British library service.* London: HMSO, 1980. (Reports 1979-80. HC 767, 409 i-iv) (ISBN 0 10 027679 2).

19. ibid. pxx.

20. DEPARTMENT OF EDUCATION AND SCIENCE OFFICE OF ARTS AND LIBRARIES. *op.cit.* Part 2, para.64.

21. ROYAL SOCIETY SCIENTIFIC INFORMATION COMMITTEE. *A study of the Scientific information system in the United Kingdom.* London: The Royal Society, 1981. (British Library Research and Development Report No.5626).

22. CABINET OFFICE. ADVISORY COUNCIL FOR APPLIED RESEARCH AND DEVELOPMENT. Information technology. London: HMSO, 1980. 56pp.

23. NATIONAL BODY: worst suspicions confirmed by minister's memo. *The Times Higher Education Supplement,* 431, 6 February 1981, p.1.

24. The University and its Finances, part II. Issued as supplementary edition of University of Bristol Newsletter, 30 October 1981.

DISCUSSION

Discussion focussed upon four main areas:

1.  What constitutes a 'centre of excellence'?  It was
    thought that the Working Party had major public libraries
    with research collections in mind, together with industrial
    libraries with special collections. University libraries
    could also be centres of excellence.

    There was some discussion about whether the British Library
    was a centre of excellence. It was thought by some that the
    British Library was hardly a 'centre'; others thought that
    the Reference Division was potentially a centre of excellence,
    but chose not to act as one because of its restrictive
    policies on access and use.

2.  Increasing costs of journals require that many subscrip-
    tions be cut. Discussion of the possibility of co-
    operative journal acquisition schemes concluded that,
    without firm guarantees that certain titles will continue
    to be taken by a particular library, such schemes are
    bound to fail, and that no library is in a position to
    offer such a guarantee.

3.  There was praise for the way in which the British Library
    had developed. The shaping of a single library system out
    of a disparate range of libraries had been a great
    achievement. It is now accepted that the British Library
    is not a co-ordinating body. The task of the Library and
    Information Services Council is to develop national policy,
    and perhaps to be a co-ordinating body: the British Library
    is simply the biggest organisation of those being co-
    ordinated. The increasing self-confidence of the British
    Library makes it more ready to accept its limitations.

4.  What is the mood of the government on charging for library
    services?  It was thought that there was no chance of the
    introduction of charges for basic public library services,
    if only for political reasons. There are services, however,
    for which charges may be approved.

# THE FRAMEWORK OF RESEARCH :
# NATIONAL DATA AND NATIONAL STATISTICS

Warwick A. Price
*Head of Library Services, Huddersfield Polytechnic*

What I should like to do this morning is to consider that hapless figure, the academic library manager as he struggles to defend his library service within an institution forced to examine critically every item of expenditure and to cut back this expenditure - often in a crisis mode. I shall go on to say something about the kinds and sources of library statistical data which he might employ by way of defence.

My concern is for a library manager in a difficulty which is, in large measure, a political difficulty. Accordingly my remarks are not concerned with methods of performance appraisal and the like but merely with the data available to guide and to support his statements and his advice to those responsible for resource allocation and for overall policy.

The library manager's difficulties are perhaps more poignant than many others'. His very purpose is to provide, on a large scale, a wide range of library materials and services to a generally vociferous and demanding clientele, and to engage in all manner of interrelated strategies to maximise the take-up and the effectiveness of these facilities in support of teaching and research. The development and the diversification of services and collection policies has been pretty well uninterrupted for some decades, and our users have come to expect a high standard of provision. In these circumstances the academic library manager has an onerous duty to protect and to defend the overall academic purpose and ethos of the library and not merely to resist in isolation the latest incursion into his bookfund or the current move to freeze a vacant post.

It is fair to say that some libraries are now facing very severe problems indeed. It is not just a matter of simply reducing expenditure. The financial decision-making chain within an institution may be involved and slow. Worse, the resulting decisions may turn out to be only provisional, possibly reflecting the unknown elements over which the committees agonise (doubt over the cost of salary increases; the unknown level of future fee income; uncertain provisions for allowances for inflation). The result may be allocation of 'half' a bookfund with little indication of what may or may not follow later. In some cases the retrenchment may be so severe as to place in doubt the ability of the library to provide even the most basic support for academic programmes. In these circumstances it is the fact that the library manager's ability to plan is removed from him that is the most worrying consequence of institutional crisis management.

It is the effects of retrenchment within the library itself, however, with which we are most concerned. How should one apply a 40% cut, in real terms, in the library's revenue fund? Should inter-library loan expenditure be reduced and the saving used to protect periodical subscriptions; or should it be maintained (or even increased) to provide an effective lifeline for the supply of needed articles? How would you justify to an anxious library committee total protection of expenditure on your new-fangled co-operative cataloguing consortium membership at the expense of funds for book and periodical purchase? What is the minimum financial requirement for monograph purchase to ensure maintenance of academic standards? Which services could safely be dispensed with? If a quarter of the library staff disappear through frozen vacancies or redundancy and services cannot be maintained, would you cut opening hours or technical services, or what? Should support of under-graduate teaching and learning have absolute priority over the needs of research? Would your answers to these questions be the same if, instead of for one year, the reduction were to apply for, say, four years? What is the likely effect of the excision of one library service on those remaining? Could the effects of a reduction in service occasioned by a squeeze on revenue be offset by an item of capital expenditure? How does one answer the temptation to cut those facilities calculated to produce the strongest reaction? Which facilities, once cut, would be difficult, or expensive, to resuscitate at a later date? Which facilities, if cut, would produce immediate savings?

I think that you will agree that library functions and services are very much interrelated. It must be axiomatic that analysis of the characteristics and dynamics of the existing situation must form part of the basis for decision if some reduction or dilution is unavoidable and a 'least damage' solution is desired. In assessing such figures and statements the library manager will have regard not only to absolute measures and trends with respect to the number of inter-library loan transactions, but also for example the interrelationships with other services, such as with the provision of an on-line bibliographic literature searching service. All this implies that the library manager presides over a sufficient and responsive data collection system within the library and, where necessary, can access data in other parts of his institution.

On this last point it is worth mentioning the generally very high proportion of total university, polytechnic and college expenditure represented by salary costs. Not all library managers necessarily know what their staff costs are and how they relate in detail to their library operation. But if they are required to make structural changes in order to reduce costs they must be able to assess both materials and staff costs attributable to various library areas. In some institutions it is apparently not at all easy to discover employment cost data. It is important to train your Finance or Bursar's Department to do this for you.

It is an understandable as well as an instinctive reaction for a library manager to compare figures illustrative of his own library situation with those of similar establishments. This looking to left and to right should not of course replace the assessment of the Librarian and his colleagues of the best way to deploy his resources. The judicious use of comparative figures can however greatly assist submissions to committees generally, although this point may have less force in a university context.

I now propose to look briefly at 'official' library statistics and then to consider more recent attempts to produce comparative figures cooperatively as working tools for library managers.

At the 'official' level then, we have volume 6 of the series *Statistics of Education* (1) which is an annual

compilation of information culled from universities' returns
to the University Grants Committee (UGC). In the most recent
volume expenditure is given by salaries, book purchase,
periodical purchase, binding costs and 'other expenditure'
for each university library for the academic year 1979/80.
I understand that this portion of *Statistics of Education*
is to be replaced by a new publication of the U.G.C. which
will present university statistics in three divisions:
student numbers and characteristics; 'first destination'
data; and finance. It remains to be seen how much university
library data will appear and how up-to-date the figures will
be.

Every other year the Department of Education and Science
asks the so-called 'public sector' establishments to provide
a range of finance, stock, staffing and other figures for
their library services. This is eventually processed and
published as *Statistics of Libraries in Major Establishments
of Further Education in England, Wales and Northern Ireland*.
(2). The latest relates equally to the academic year 1979/1980.

Whilst useful to trace past trends in a number of areas,
these compilations fall short of what is needed to assist
the problem solving activities of library managers; indeed
they are not really compiled with this in mind. In another
discipline A.H. Halsey observed:

> 'the problem remains largely that of adapting to social
> science ends statistics which, from the point of view of
> the sociologist, are a by-product of administrative or
> organizational activity.' (3)

The biggest single drawback of these official statistics is
that they are well out of date.

In recent years both SCONUL (Standing Conference of
National and University Libraries) and its younger relation
COPOL (Council of Polytechnic Librarians) have been paying
more attention to the provision of statistics for the use
of member librarians. Both bodies have committees working
in this area.

SCONUL have revised and enhanced their previous questionnaire undertaken jointly with the Library Association and
now produce sets of ratios as well as a range of absolute
figures. These show categories of expenditure expressed as a
proportion of total library spending and in the form of

expenditure per student. SCONUL also survey and circulate to their members details of the effects of cuts, frozen posts etc., usually on a semi-annual basis. SCONUL's broadsheet, *SCONULOG*, comments on the current situation in a recent issue:

'The first trial tabulation of university expenditure statistics was reviewed and received by members with satisfaction. A new and more comprehensive collection of this data has been undertaken on behalf of SCONUL by the University of St. Andrews, where the computer has been programmed to produce tabulations of ratios which it is hoped will be helpful to Representatives in the monitoring of trends. Some of the general tables are being made available to the Publishers Association and it is hoped that this more comprehensive collection will enable institutions to complete a number of requests for data without further work. The Library Association has indicated its willingness to use this data in place of the returns made to the joint SCONUL/LA annual questionnaire'. (4)

SCONUL's general motivation and approach seems to me to resemble closely that of COPOL, and I should like to take a closer look at COPOL's work in statistics.

The Council of Polytechnic Librarians has produced an annual staffing survey for a good number of years. This shows the FTE number and grading of all library staff posts in 31 polytechnic libraries. The data is available to members a month or two after the 'snapshot' is taken and can be used by members in staffing negotiations whilst the data remains reliable. We analyse the total trends in staff numbers as well as the incidence of frozen posts and posts deleted over the previous year. We also attempt, though at present only crudely, to plot the number and subject coverage of each staffed library service point within each polytechnic and to show the number of staff deployed in each. Staff organisation diagrams are also being pooled and circulated to members.

We have also monitored bookfund trends each year and have usually followed up with mid-year surveys to keep abreast with what is, these days, often a very fluid situation. A further analysis is made by way of isolating those categories of purchase (books, stationery etc.) which are met from 'bookfund' and those which are not. In addition members report on any other 'earmarked' funds which they receive for particular purposes (e.g. for travel and subsistence, or for automation expenses). Further, we show those areas of expenditure where a library has no funds but must compete for monies contained in a global institutional vote (e.g. for furniture). Finally we ask members to indicate plans and allocations for capital expenditure.

We have had an informal arrangement with the organisers of the biennial survey conducted by the Department of Education and Science (DES) whereby we receive copies of institutions' returns and process these for our own purposes. The result is the circulation to member librarians of *Statistics of Polytechnic Libraries* (5). In these tables we show a range of absolute figures for each library (stock size by category; expenditure by categories; interloans; number of service points; staffing; floor areas; seating provision and other measures).

I shall attempt some assessment of all this information.

1. All three approaches (i.e. staff survey, bookfund analysis and the DES type survey of the year just ended) are all sufficiently up-to-date to be useful.

2. Whilst the matter of describing student numbers in FTE terms in the Polytechnic sector is a minefield, we do now collect polytechnics' FTE student figures on an agreed basis and use them to derive ratios in all three areas of statistical enquiry.

3. I think that you may have discerned from my description that we are, in effect, developing a 'snapshot' or 'profile' of individual polytechnic libraries of a broadly statistical character. This should permit librarians to develop an informed awareness of the character of each other's library situation. By reference and cross-reference to these 'profiles' it becomes possible to relate one library to another and to the sector as a whole. This can be a useful aid in a variety of problem solving situations.

4. One of our motives has been to make use of the more 'formal' figures to defend the polytechnic library sector in public.

So far as our public face is concerned I do think it important that we seek to project a SCONUL or a COPOL view in library statistics. There is otherwise a danger that other agencies do it for us, and don't do it very well. In this connection it is pleasing to report an informal approach from the Office for Arts and Libraries concerning the nature of statistical information which might be included in the proposed annual report to Parliament on library services.

I think that people are now generally aware of the Inter-Library Comparisons exercise. The Centre for Interfirm Comparison is concerned with the collection of financial and other data which illustrate the activity and performance of, for example, a group of manufacturing firms in a particular product area, and the manipulation of this data to produce ratios. The Centre has received contracts from the British Library to develop a model for translating this approach to libraries. Following an exercise in the public library field (6) the Centre conducted a 'Test Comparison for Academic Libraries', has issued the findings to the participants and, with their permission, is about to publish the results (7). The broad approach is not too distant from that which SCONUL and COPOL are trying to pursue. Eight polytechnic and twelve university libraries participated in the Test Comparison in 1981.

It would be tedious to describe in detail the nature of this recent 'Test Comparison'. Briefly, however, the partici- pating librarians submitted a wide range of salary, expenditure, staffing and other data on an agreed basis. The Centre for Interfirm Comparison was concerned to manipulate the data to produce measures of library functions on a comparative basis. The Centre describes the purpose as follows:

  'The objective of inter-library comparisons is to help
  those involved in the practice of library management
  through the organised pooling of comparative information.
  This information gives external yardsticks, based on the
  actual experience of other library systems, which a
  librarian can use as a management tool to help him
  evaluate the activities of his own library.

  The yardsticks help library management to see:

  how they compare in the operation of various important
  activities;

  where and why there are differences, and hence

  what scope there may be for improving services and for
  the control of costs, and the most fruitful lines along
  which action may be taken.

The information provided will enable participants to see how their allocation of resources between stock acquisition and operational expenditure compares with other libraries; how operational resources are distributed between the various functions and services: and what output is being achieved with the resources applied' (8).

An example of the results is shown as Appendix One, where cataloguing costs are analysed for the polytechnic libraries (libraries A to H) which participated.

I do hope that I have not claimed too much for 'national' library statistics. One writer describes statistics as 'a body of methods for making wise decisions in the face of uncertainty', and even this claim may need to be toned down.

My dictionary gives two usages for the verb *retrench*. One is 'cut down, reduce amount of, make excisions of, introduce economies'. We are becoming familiar with this usage. The second one reads 'furnish with inner line of defence, usually consisting of trench and parapet'. Perhaps we can interpret this as a modest falling back to build a stronger and more enduring fortification or citadel. I like to think that better library statistics will be a part of these defences. As for the parapet – that is presumably for jumping off into the arms of the barbarians. Let us hope that we do not get to that stage.

REFERENCES

1.  DEPARTMENT OF EDUCATION AND SCIENCE. *Statistics of education*. London: HMSO. Vol.6, Universities. Annual.

2.  DEPARTMENT OF EDUCATION AND SCIENCE. *Statistics of libraries of major establishments of further education in England, Wales and Northern Ireland*. London: Department of Education and Science. Bi-ennial.

3.  HALSEY, A.H. *Trends in British society since 1900*. London: Macmillan, 1972. p.3.

4.  *Sconulog*, 24 May 1982, p.2.

5.  COUNCIL OF POLYTECHNIC LIBRARIANS. *Statistics of polytechnic libraries*. (Private circulation to members).

6.  CENTRE FOR INTERFIRM COMPARISON. *Inter-library comparisons: pilot comparison with public libraries.* London: British Library, 1981. (Research and Development Report No. 5638).

7.  The report on the Centre for Interfirm Comparison's test comparisons with academic libraries is in press, and will appear in the British Library's Research and Development Report series.

8.  Extracts from the Introduction to the 'Report to participants' in Reference 7.

INTER LIBRARY COMPARISON FOR ACADEMIC LIBRARIES (Extract from Appendix 1: 'Polytechnic Library Results', Section 5)

| Ratio | Library | A | B | C | D | E | F | G | H | High | Med. | Low |
|---|---|---|---|---|---|---|---|---|---|---|---|---|
| COST OF CATALOGUING (£ per title catalogued) | | | | | | | | | | | | |
| 1) Professional Librarians | £ | 3.33 | 5.81 | 1.67 | 4.00 | 2.27 | 1.33 | 3.87 | 2.19 | 5.81 | 2.80 | 1.33 |
| 2) Library Assistants | £ | 0.96 | 0.57 | - | 1.01 | 0.95 | 0.14 | 0.51 | 0.9 | 1.01 | 0.75 | - |
| 3) Other Library Staff | £ | 0.19 | - | - | - | 0.45 | - | 0.39 | - | 0.45 | - | - |
| 4) Total Staff | £ | 4.48 | 6.38 | 1.67 | 5.01 | 3.67 | 1.47 | 4.77 | 3.11 | 6.38 | 4.08 | 1.47 |
| 5a) Cataloguing Charges - computer | £ | 0.91+ | 1.07+ | 0.63 | - | 0.76 | 0.36 | 1.46+ | 0.59 | | 0.59 | - |
| b)   - manual | £ | - | - | 0.03 | - | - | - | - | - | 0.03 | - | - |
| 6a) Catalogue production charges | | | | | | | | | | | | |
|   - computer | £ | + | + | - | - | 0.31 | 0.19 | + | 0.11 | | 0.11 | - |
| b)   - manual | £ | - | - | 0.04 | - | - | - | - | - | 0.04 | - | - |
| 7) Other costs | £ | 0.11 | 0.68 | - | - | - | 0.91 | - | - | 0.91 | - | - |
| TOTAL | £ | 5.50 | 8.13 | 2.37 | 5.01 | 4.74 | 2.93 | 6.23 | 3.81 | 8.13 | 4.88 | 2.37 |

DISCUSSION

The discussion centred upon the following points:

1. The British Library, while not being able to provide
   further financial support for comparative studies, was
   anxious both to disseminate the results of the present
   study and to encourage the appropriate organizations -
   SCONUL and COPOL - to continue this sort of work on their
   own.

2. The statistics required by various bodies - DES, SCONUL,
   COPOL, UGC, etc. - are often not readily available and
   are, when supplied, often not reliable. It is easier to
   keep reliable figures if they are kept on a continuing
   or recurring basis. Automation is not the answer.

3. The organisations and institutions involved should have
   some part in determining the statistics that are to be
   collected and the way in which they are to be collected.

4. Statistics should be accompanied by background material
   that would make a more thorough appreciation possible of
   the difference between one institution and another.
   Anonymity in the presentation of statistics was generally
   regarded as unhelpful, both because institutions can
   usually be identified and because comparisons are only
   useful if more knowledge about the institutions being
   compared can be brought to bear.

5. Although some thought that unreliable statistics had their
   place in negotiations within an institution, it was pointed
   out that statistics were used by people other than those
   managing the institutions represented by the statistics,
   so they should be as accurate as possible.

6. There was talk about the kinds of qualitative measures of
   library performance that were desirable or possible.
   Questions about the real contribution of the library to
   teaching, learning and research had to be faced.

# THE FRAMEWORK OF RESEARCH :
# IN-HOUSE RESEARCH

Geoffrey Ford
*Sub-Librarian, University of Southampton*

For the purposes of this paper, in-house research is
defined as the investigation of activity in a library system,
the results of which will assist in the solution of a management problem. I regard research or investigation as fundamental
to management. Management is all about information and control.
In order to control you need information. Some of that information which is collected regularly; some is needed less often,
but does require some intellectual effort and commitment of
resources. It is this latter type of information gathering
exercise with which I am principally concerned. The need for
management information may arise from the results of an *ad hoc*
investigation: perhaps because the usefulness of such
information has been demonstrated, or because there is a need
to monitor the effects of some innovation resulting from a
research project.

Investigation, then, should be continuous but selective.
How should it be implemented? The tradition in libraries is
to conduct a survey which is usually imperfectly designed,
and in consequence, the data collected is inadequately analysed
and the results when presented are difficult to interpret.
There are several reasons for this, one being that librarians
may not have been given training in social research techniques
nor in practical management. Many people do not appreciate the
differences between research designed to prove or disprove
hypotheses on the one hand, and investigation designed to give
insights on the other.

It is important here to digress a little into the differences between these two modes of research. A fuller treatment can be found in Martyn and Lancaster (1). The 'proof oriented' approach starts by setting up a hypothesis and then seeks to prove it or disprove it under controlled conditions. The 'insight oriented' approach is less complex and cheaper and is analogous to a series of raids designed to show how experimental variables interact with one another. Even where the proof-oriented approach is used the results may not be worth having. One may examine the effectiveness of different filing strategies in a card catalogue and discover that strategy A is better than strategy B under given conditions. The next step is to determine whether the given conditions are realistic, how much better is A than B, and is the difference enough to matter.

A further point, on the economics of investigation, is that several small studies giving insights could be carried out for the same price as one proof-oriented test, and the observed results might say a lot more about the system being investigated than any single experiment. The thrust of a manager's investigations should be to discover why users and systems behave in certain ways and thus to suggest how systems can be made more effective.

The results of any study need careful interpretation and there may be more than one interpretation of the same set of facts. An example relates to the borrowing habits of students of different disciplines. In the late 1950s and early 1960s several studies (2,3,4) showed that Arts students borrowed more books than Social Science students, who in turn borrowed more than Scientists (Table 1).

Table 1: Undergraduate borrowing in university libraries

(Loans per student)

|  | (1)<br>Birmingham | (2)<br>Leeds | (3)<br>Sheffield |
|---|---|---|---|
| Arts | 17.0 | ) | 21.0 |
| Social Science | 14.0 | )17.89 | 18.2 |
| Science | 10.0 | )<br>10.76 | 8.1 |

These results might be explained by suggesting that Arts people need to read more books because they are studying the written records of human activity whereas Scientists are studying natural phenomena and thus work in laboratories. Social Science is a hybrid of Arts and Science, and therefore it is not surprising if Social Scientists read more than Scientists and less than Arts people. That is one chain of reasoning.

An alternative chain might be that one purpose of higher education is to train people in the techniques which will enable them to carry out research in their chosen field. Scientists need to be able to carry out experiments so time is spent in training them in these techniques. Arts people on the whole can only study written records, and so education is based on a critical examination of those records. However, given the vast amount of scientific knowledge that exists, it is arguable that a Scientist needs to read at least as much as an Arts person, if not more, to avoid needlessly replicating existing research, and so that his own research can be placed in the context of existing work and perhaps more meaningfully interpreted. The reason why Scientists borrow fewer books is *not* that they do not need to, but that the amount of experimental training they receive does not leave them enough time to read. There is a basic educational problem here which needs co-operation with teaching staff if the library is to contribute to the solution.

A more interesting phenomenon is the difference in borrowing rates between libraries in different institutions. Table 2 shows the range in a number of universities which are broadly comparable in terms of the proportion of students reading Arts based subjects, and are generally comparable in terms of the Faculties they contain. At Nottingham, twice as many books were borrowed as at Glasgow. We see that Nottingham users occupy seats 50% more often than those at Glasgow: and library expenditure is roughly the same at both places. There does not seem to be any particular pattern in these figures. The major variable appears to be loan policy.

It is not necessary to repeat the well-known arguments about the variables in loan policy. Most of the variables have been covered adequately in the early work at Lancaster University by Buckland and Hindle (5). The principal factors which they did not consider were the effect of fines on the return pattern of books and the effect of an absolute limitation

Table 2: Borrowing rates and other indices

| University | % of students reading Arts subjects | No. of loans per FTE student | Average seat occupancy per FTE student x100 | Expenditure per FTE student £ |
|---|---|---|---|---|
| Leeds | 44.4 | 47 | 10.6 | 128 |
| Liverpool | 43.1 | 42 | N.A. | 149 |
| Nottingham | 42.4 | 49 | 9.3 | 147 |
| Sheffield | 46.1 | 43 | 3.0 | 143 |
| Southampton | 44.3 | 32 | 8.1 | 170 |
| Glasgow | 46.1 | 25 | 6.0 | 148 |

Source: U.G.C. returns; Annual reports of university libraries

on the number of books which could be borrowed. It has
subsequently been shown by Ford and others (6) that the
imposition of fines increases the proportion of books returned
on time, and by Winkworth (7) that a limitation on the number
of loans permitted is more likely to inhibit the individual
borrower than to seriously affect the overall availability of
books to other users. One must remember that the analytical
work on loan policy at Lancaster University was inspired by
the search for an adequate performance measure for libraries,
and it was thought that 'satisfaction level' was the single
most useful measure of library performance that could be
devised. Although the term is a good one, the operational
formulation of satisfaction level used, which related to the
probability that readers would obtain the books they wanted,
is faulty.

Subsequent work at Lancaster University by Buckland (8)
showed that satisfaction level, as defined, was apparently
homeostatic. That is to say, a change in policy could lead
to an increase in satisfaction level, but then demand would
increase and thus bring the level down to its previous figure.
In several academic libraries it has been noted by Buckland
and others (9), Urquhart and Schofield (10), and Harris and
Forer (11) that satisfaction level is around 60%. Any library
can measure their own satisfaction level by using the standard
technique developed by the Library Management Research Unit
(LMRU), subsequently the Centre for Library and Information
Management (CLAIM) (12).

We therefore need to look for different measures of
performance. I regard it as axiomatic that a library is always
part of a larger system. A library, like any other organisation,
must be seen as part of a political system which includes, at
the very least, its users and its source of funds.

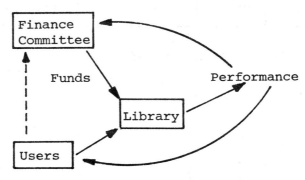

Fig. 1: The library in a larger system

Figure 1 is a simple-minded representation of the links between the library, its users and its source of funds. The users place demands on the library and the performance of the library feeds back into the users, who may themselves influence the source of funds. It is easy to see that because a library is part of a larger system, the library's objectives must relate to that larger system. In order to evaluate a library service, the performance of the service must be related to the objectives. It is clear that we should be concerned to measure the impact of the service which we are attempting to evaluate.

The easiest things to measure are, of course, inputs which are reported to the Department of Education and Science (DES) and the University Grants Committee (UGC) and printed in *Statistics of Education* (34) and elsewhere. Warwick Price has already dealt appropriately with this sort of input statistic (Table 3).

Table 3: Some input measures

| Library | Expenditure (£000s) | | | Average cost per document metre added to stock (£) |
|---------|-------|-------------|-------|----------------|
| | Books | Periodicals | Other | |
| Leeds | 345 | 169 | 149 | 440 |
| Liverpool | 203 | 206 | 73 | NA |
| Nottingham | 145 | 179 | 67 | 380 |
| Sheffield | 201 | 180 | 137 | 360 |
| Southampton | 179 | 157 | 125 | 390 |
| Glasgow | 239 | 190 | 141 | 400 |

Source: U.G.C. returns 1978-79

Some outputs are also fairly easy to measure, and library
annual reports are full of figures relating to outputs, such
as number of loans, number of readers 'introduced' to the
library and so on. Much research in libraries is concerned
with attempting to relate output with impact. The reason for
this is that the measurement of impact is extremely difficult.
The search continues for an output measure that acts as a
predictor for an impact measure.

Remembering that measures should relate to objectives, let
us suppose that the objective of the library is to support
the research programme of the university. How might the impact
of a library's policies directed towards that objective be
measured? The norm is to take an output measure which seems
likely to be relevant. For example, a document delivery test
might be used to measure the ability of the library to support
research in a given field. Table 4 gives some results from
one such test.

Table 4:   Effectiveness of libraries for research

| Library | Chemistry | Geography |
|---------|-----------|-----------|
| A | 75 | 29 |
| B | 89 | 57 |
| C | 94 | 63 |
| D | 79 | 52 |
| E | 85 | 31 |
| F | 93 | 85 |

*Source:* unpublished research results

The figures represent the percentages of documents, cited in
a group of PhD theses, which were available in a number of
university libraries.

Document delivery tests are, however, difficult to carry
out. An alternative might be to take a simpler output measure,
and look at the annual acquisition rate in those subjects.
Table 5 shows how two libraries can have very similar
acquisition rates and yet not be equally effective in meeting
research needs.

Table 5:   Acquisition rates and effectiveness

|  | Sussex University | | Southampton University | |
|---|---|---|---|---|
| Subject | % increase in stock 1969/79 | Research effectiveness | % increase in stock 1969/79 | Research effectiven |
| English | 89 | ca 75 | 35 | ca 50 |
| Economics | 81 | ca 75 | 77 | ca 50 |

Research effectiveness: % of PhD citations found in libraries
Source: unpublished research

These results need to be interpreted with caution. It is worth noting that at Southampton University, the acquisitions policy fo English Literature does not seek to meet research needs, but is aimed specifically at meeting teaching needs. It should not be surprising therefore if research needs are less well met than might be desirable.

So far this paper has concentrated on the theory of in-house research. To turn to practicalities, in-house research should assist in solving management problems. What are the problems of management?  More particularly, what are the problems of retrenchment?  Management problems can be grouped into five main categories:

Political

Stock Control

Marketing

Processing

Administration

POLITICAL

It may be necessary to do some research for political reasons, to counter for example, arguments that inter-library loan is very expensive and should be scrapped or that

departmental libraries are essential to the efficient
functioning of various departments. One may also need to
undertake research in the library to show that it is no
different from other libraries. Every institution has pet
practices and beliefs. It may be necessary to support
innovations by undertaking an investigation to convince both
library staff and users that a new loan policy or form of
catalogue is feasible. I regard this kind of research as
politically motivated. It is necessary because the great
majority of staff and users have too little experience of
other institutions.


STOCK CONTROL

The considerations of objective setting, goals and
performance measurement are well illustrated by the three
main areas of stock control:


Selection policy

Weeding

Loan policy

How can the effectiveness of a selection policy be measured?
One measure might be the number of books which have to be
discarded owing to lack of use. However the amount of use of
a group of books can be influenced by the loan policy in
operation. In addition, the teaching and research activity
of the institution is a largely uncontrollable factor which
influences the whole area.

The ideal towards which we strive can be expressed in terms
of thresholds of use. If a book fails to achieve a defined,
low level of use, discard it; if it achieves a defined, high
level, of use, buy an extra copy. In the ideal world we would
be able to predict whether or not a book will achieve a
certain level of use before we buy it and act accordingly.
The fact that we are not in an ideal world is shown by Table
6.

Table 6:  Relative effectiveness of acquisitions policies

| Subject | Year of Acquisition | Percentage still not used by 1979 | |
|---------|---------------------|-----------------------------------|---|
| | | Southampton Univ. | Sussex Univ. |
| Economics | 1969-70 | 25 | 30 |

In order to find a suitable measure in this area appropriate data must be collected - but which data?  What insights can we gain from elsewhere?

    Assume for the moment that we are interested in the effectiveness of our stock control policy for economics. Figure 2 is a Venn diagram showing the relationship of various relevant groups of books. Economists often explain supply and demand in terms of apples, oranges and sundry other fruits, hence their use here.

Fig.2:  Venn diagram for economists

The apple represents the items selected and acquired as being relevant to the teaching and research in economics. The orange represents the items classified as economics according to the library's classification scheme. The lemon represents the books used by economists. How can this help in measuring the success of our stock control policy?  It is quite clear that we shall not get very far by merely looking at the use or non-use of the oranges - the items classified as economics. What insights can be gleaned from elsewhere?

Let us assume that we are trying to ensure that our library, which is not primarily archival, contains a minimal amount of useless material. An item which has not been used within fifty years of its acquisition is, *prima facie*, useless, because it has not been used during the professional life of the person who selected it. How can use be measured? A variety of studies have shown that a considerable amount of the use of library materials is normally not recorded.

Table 7:   In-library use and borrowing

| Library | Rates of in library use/borrowing |
|---|---|
| Durham University | 5 |
| Lancaster University | 4.5 |
| Newcastle Polytechnic | 5 |

References: Ford (13), unpublished data, Harris (14)

It is very expensive to mount a study of in-library use, and in the short term the data are liable to manipulation by mischievous users. From the work of Ford (13), Harris (14), Fussler and Simon (15) and Hindle (16) in this field, we can state that for every book borrowed in a given time period, on average, five more may be used in the library (there are wide variations between subjects); and that, at any given time, the books used in the library tend to be those which have recently been on loan. Thus, in general, we may, leaving aside the *usefulness* of use, refer to borrowing histories as a guide to the usefulness of individual books.

Turning to borrowing statistics, these may be analysed in order to predict the future, using mathematical models which need not be very sophisticated. For example, the following very simple model was used successfully in the late 1960s to predict both the amount of loan traffic and the intensity of library use.

$$\frac{\text{Number of students next year}}{\text{Number of students this year}} = \frac{\text{Extent of activity next year}}{\text{Extent of activity this year}}$$

The results of applying this model are shown in the following table.

Table 8: Prediction of library use

|  | Predictions | Actual |
|---|---|---|
| Loans | 13790 | 13980 |
| Highest daily no. of users | 1165 | 1180 |
| Highest weekly no. of users | 6160 | 6010 |

Source: Ford (17)

More complex models are required if we are to look further into the future. See, for example, Burrell (18, 19), Burrell and Cane (20) and Hindle and Worthington (21). Some of these models have formulations which look rather formidable to the non-mathematician. However, it is reassuring to be able to refer to one eminent statistician and former member of the University Grants Committee (22) who has pointed out that in practice many models cannot be distinguished. That is to say, having collected data and plotted graphs, you are free to choose whichever formulation best suits your purpose. The simplest model quoted by Burrell (19) requires the estimation of just two parameters - the proportion of active items in a library's stock, and the average number of loans per item per unit time. These parameters can be estimated quite simply from the kind of data on loans which are easily generated from automated circulation systems.

This type of model can be applied to the fairly common problem of storage space. For example, Sussex University Library is becoming overcrowded. How much material can be safely thrown away to make room for more? With regard to the cost of storing books, one set of calculations implies

that it is cheaper to keep them on site if they are expected
to be used at least once in the next thirty years (20). At
Sussex the only books which can be expected to be used less
often than this are those which have not been borrowed since
1962. At the end of 1962 there were only 32,836 books in
stock, so that is the *maximum* number which can be discarded.
In practice the number which can be discarded will be lower
since many of those books will have been used since 1962.
Given an annual acquisition rate of 10,000 items, Sussex
University can buy themselves, at most, three years worth of
shelf space by having a weeding exercise now. The time bought
could be as low as six months. Any greater amount of weeding
is liable to be less cost-effective than building a store.

Sussex University has been used as an example because they
have collected data on use through their automated circulation
system for a number of years, and the existence of that data
on the borrowing histories of individual books helped in the
formulation of the simple model mentioned earlier. Libraries
which accumulate borrowing data can estimate for their own
library the likelihood that weeding low-use material will gain
significant amounts of space.

*Inter-library loans*

Is it reasonable to rely on inter-library loan for books
which have been discarded, or never purchased?  Some users
think inter-library loan is expensive, as do some librarians.
We know from a number of studies that for most users the
inter-library loan service delivers books quickly enough for
them to be of use (23, 24, 25).

Given that delays are a significant factor, it is reasonable
to discuss the acquisition versus inter-library loan question
in terms of cost. How often should a book be used over what
time period for it to be worth buying?  It is now thirteen
years since the *Project for evaluating the benefits from
University libraries* (PEBUL) Report showed that a book should
only be purchased if it was going to be borrowed five times
during its life in the library (26). At that time it was
reasonable to ignore storage costs since capital money seemed
to be more freely available. The calculations need repeating,
partly because more people are now aware of storage costs,
partly because the real cost of inter-library loan has risen.
A further reason is that in-library use was ignored in the

PEBUL calculation.

It is quite clear that buying a book and then waiting for
twenty years to see if it is going to be borrowed once is
(a) time consuming and (b) potentially wasteful, but there
do not seem to be any short cuts. While it seems likely that
a book which is in high demand during its first year of use
continues to be heavily used for at least the next ten years,
there is no correlation between the rate of use of a given
book and the likelihood that it will become inactive (unpublished
data from Sussex and Southampton University Libraries (20)). It is
true that in a given year, 20% of the stock gives rise to
80% of the use; but over longer periods of time a larger
proportion of stock comes into use, and there are wide
variations between subjects. The number of potential readers
and the number of books acquired are important variables and
further statistical work is needed in this area. We need to
try to predict at the time at which a book is acquired the
likelihood that it will be used. An early attempt was made
at Lancaster University, whilst more recently the City of
London Polytechnic Library and the Centre for Library and
Information Management have initiated a longitudinal study
in which variables are characterised at the time of acquisition,
(Table 9) to be correlated with the use of the book in
succeeding years.

Table 9: Possible predictors of use of books

| Data Element | MARC Tag |
|---|---|
| Country of Publication | 008$b |
| Edition | 250$a |
| Price | local tag |
| Form | 008$d or $p |
| Subject | 050, 080, or 082 or local tag |
| Author notoriety | |
| On reading list | local tag |
| Size of publisher | from ISBN? |
| Selector | local tag |

Source: Payne (27)

Some of these data would be readily obtainable from an automated acquisitions and cataloguing system, others require judgments to be made. When this study is reported on, it will be important to assess the sensitivity of the results to the measure chosen for the qualitative variables.

The desirable aim for stock control is a decision table (Figure 3). If the expected level of use per year is <X, rely on inter-library loan, if ⩾X buy, and if ⩾Y, buy duplicates. Between X and Y there are two further thresholds (P and Q) which can be used to define loan periods.

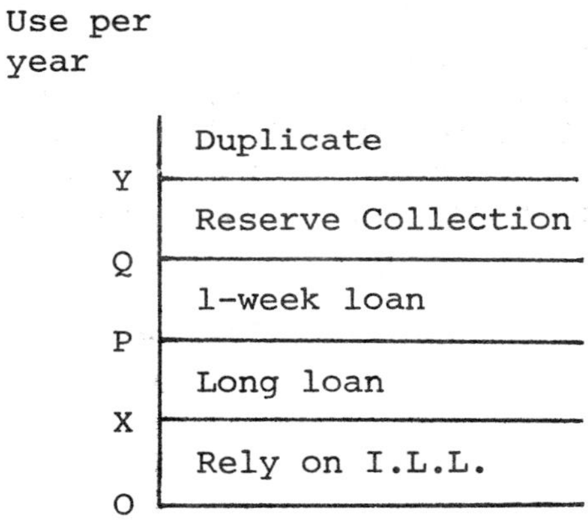

Use per
year

| | |
|---|---|
| Y | Duplicate |
| Q | Reserve Collection |
| P | 1-week loan |
| X | Long loan |
| O | Rely on I.L.L. |

Fig. 3: Thresholds of use

Estimates for these thresholds would be:

X = 0.1 (ie., 1 use in 10 years)

P = 4

Q = 10

Y = 16

It would be useful to hear of anyone who has empirical data which will refute or confirm these figures.

A related and unpopular activity related to stock control is stock taking. In a recent article Kohl (28) has shown that the rate of loss from a given subject area is positively correlated with the rate of use of the stock and the percentage reported missing by the users. For libraries with appropriate data, this should be followed up, as it gives a short cut to identifying the areas which are worth the committment of man-power to stocktaking; another contribution to our programme of retrenchment.

MARKETING OR STOCK EXPLOITATION

Under this heading we may group user education, advertising and library guiding, none of which have been convincingly demonstrated as having any lasting effect on the users. There is plenty of anecdotal evidence to show that users do not read notices and that standard forms of user education do not have much effect. To be effective, it seems that user education needs to relate to a particular task which the user has to do, and that the method of instruction needs to be related, not only to that task, but to the personality of the user (Figure 4).

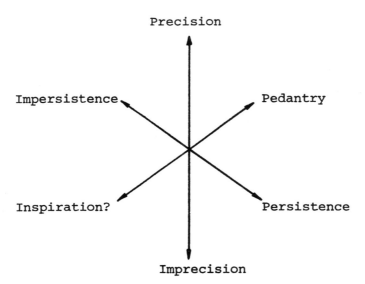

Fig. 4: P - I scales

We can consider that the user who has a task to fulfil will have a need which can be placed on a scale of Precision. At one end he needs a very precise piece of information such as the properties of a recently synthesized chemical compound. Only one source of information exists. At the other, he needs some details of the life of Queen Victoria. Any number of sources exist for this information, so the need is imprecise. The method of finding that information will depend on two personality factors - the persistence of the individual, and the degree of pedantry of his approach to the problem.

In general, library regulations, guides and notices are based on the assumption that users are all persistent pedants. They go from the name catalogue to the plan of the library and from the plan to the shelves. If they do not find what they want they use the classified catalogue to find other works on the same subject and go back to the shelves. If they really want a book they will use the reservation system, and their fellow users will receive, read and respond to recall notices. This is the syndrome known as Librarian's Fiction.

There is ample evidence in the literature which shows that much formal library education is wasted, and a superfluity of observational evidence that the bulk of library users are neither persistent nor pedantic in their approach. It is rare to find a library which has a consistent marketing policy which takes note of the true nature of users, but more common to find notices and guides which read *The symbol 'Q' in the middle of a class-mark to indicate geographical sub-division of a subject ... represents the figures '09' and is so filed. Other letters occurring in classmarks are filed in normal alphabetical sequence.* That is a most telling argument for encouraging library catalogues and notations to be designed by those who have to explain them to the readers and not by pure-bred cataloguers.

Since, during retrenchment, libraries have to cut back on staff, it is even more important that librarians should make their libraries easier to use by the uninitiated. This means that the number of sequences on the shelves should be minimised. How many users know of the existence of pamphlet, quarto, folio and elephant folio sequences, or the variations of 'stack', 'secure stack', 'reference', 'locked case' etc. The layout of catalogues should be simple, with built in explanations, and guiding must be simple and direct, with colour coding re-inforcing rather than replacing essential information. Other institutions can offer valuable insights in this area. Reynolds (29), for example, shows how simple changes in layout can affect the readability of microfiche catalogues. Increasing readability must increase use, and librarians can benefit by applying the results of such work to improving their own records to which users have access. The work of the Centre for Catalogue Research at Bath University provides many insights into the sort of catalogue records which would satisfy the vast bulk of users' needs. Elaborate research does not seem to be necessary but insights are needed and these can be obtained from independent observers. Southampton University Library has used two newly arrived non-librarians to locate a number of items in the library. A subsequent guiding system will be based on their report.


PROCESSING

The acquisition, cataloguing and loan procedures which comprise this area of management need regular review. They are the activities most susceptible to the production of output statistics - items catalogued per day, loans processed per assistant, etc. It is these essential activities which are least well understood by users, academic colleagues, and political masters. The constant demand for more productivity can only be reached by:

1)    Using new technology

2)    Concentrating on what you do best

3)    Streamlining procedures

4)    Reducing staff numbers

In this context the Centre for Catalogue Research has shown how reducing the content of catalogue entries can reduce costs while increasing effectiveness (30). Southampton University Library has based its catalogue design and production policy partly on the work of the Centre.

ADMINISTRATION

Budgeting, staffing and space planning can be included under this heading. Can in-house research help with these activities?  Little research exists which will assist the manager to bestir those of his staff who have taken root. However, there are some interesting studies on library space (31, 32, 33).

One area of budgeting - the allocation of funds for the purchase of library materials - is of particular importance. Allied with stock control it is central to a library's business and worth the devotion of considerable effort. Many academic libraries rely on teaching staff to select books for stock, but how many try to find out what criteria the staff are using to select, what balance, if any, there is between provision for teaching and research, or between books and periodicals?  This is the kind of research which can only be done in-house.

With regard to periodicals one can derive from the litera-ture that, in general, one cannot use other people's lists of popular periodicals in order to judge one's own needs. There is no easy route to the cancellation of subscriptions. Studies at Southampton University Library have shown that as few as two 'current' uses per issue are sufficient to justify subscribing to a periodical rather than relying on inter-library loan.

We all recognise that in one sense a library is part of a larger system. In another sense it is also part of a second system, that which includes all libraries of the same general type. There is no great difference between the people who use one academic library as opposed to those who use another. A careful library manager can draw on experience gained elsewhere and apply it in his own situation. He can look at the results of research in other institutions and derive insights which will enable him to compare himself with others. This cumulation of insights is probably the most valuable result of in-house research, provided it is published. Libraries such as those at the City of London and Newcastle upon Tyne Polytechnics, which published lists of their internal reports and make them available, are to be commended and emulated wherever possible.

The brief for this paper was to assess the potential of in-house research and review the different styles and models together with the possibilities of cumulation and comparison between institutions. I hope that some of the examples given and comments made have illuminated these points.

REFERENCES

1. MARTYN, J. and LANCASTER, F.W. *Investigative methods in library and information science: an introduction.* Arlington: Information Resources Press, 1981.

2. HUMPHREYS, K.W. Survey of borrowing from the main library, the University of Birmingham. *Libri,* 14(2), 1964, 126-35.

3. PAGE, B.S. and TUCKER, P.E. The Nuffield pilot survey of library use in the University of Leeds. *Journal of Documentation,* 15(1), March 1959, 1-11.

4. SAUNDERS, W.L. *et al.* Survey of borrowing from the University of Sheffield Library during one academic year. *In:* Saunders, W.L. *(ed). The provision and use of library and documentation services.* Oxford: Pergamon, 1966, pp.115-43.

5. BUCKLAND, M.K. and HINDLE, A. Loan policies, duplication and availability. *In:* Mackenzie, A.G. *and* Stuart, I.M. *(eds). Planning library services.* Lancaster: University of Lancaster Library, 1965 (University of Lancaster Library Occasional Papers, 3).

6. FORD, G. *et al. Report on circulation prepared for the SWULSCP Working Party.* Bristol: South-West Universities Library Systems Cooperation Project, 1971.

7. WINKWORTH, I. *How restrictive are limits on the number of books a borrower may have at one time?* Newcastle: Newcastle upon Tyne Polytechnic Library, 1980 (Planning and Research Note, 18).

8. BUCKLAND, M.K. *Book availability and the library user.* Oxford: Pergamon, 1975.

9.  BUCKLAND, M.K. *et al. Systems analysis of a university library.* Lancaster: University of Lancaster Library, 1970. (University of Lancaster Library Occasional Papers, 4).

10. URQUHART, J.A. and SCHOFIELD, J.L. Measuring readers' failure at the shelf in three university libraries. *Journal of Documentation,* 28(3), September 1972, 233-41.

11. HARRIS, F. and FORER, J. *Southampton University Library: graduate trainee project, 1979/80* (Unpublished).

12. CENTRE FOR LIBRARY AND INFORMATION MANAGEMENT. *Reader failure at the shelf.* Loughborough: Centre for Library and Information Management, 1982. (Aids to Library Administration, 2).

13. FORD, G. Surveys of unrecorded use. *In: Project for evaluating the benefits from university libraries. Final report.* Durham: University of Durham Computer Unit, 1969. (Appendix 8). (OSTI Report No. 5056).

14. HARRIS, C. A comparison of issues and in-library use of books. *Aslib Proceedings,* 29(3), March 1977, 118-26.

15. FUSSLER, H.H. and SIMON, J.L. *Patterns in the use of books in large research libraries.* Chicago: University of Chicago Library, 1961.

16. HINDLE, A. *Developing an acquisitions system for a university library.* London: British Library, 1977. (Research and Development Report No.5351).

17. FORD, G. Data collection and feedback. *In:* Mackenzie, A.G. and Stuart, I.M. *(eds). Planning library services.* Lancaster: University of Lancaster Library, 1969. (University of Lancaster Library Occasional Papers, 3).

18. BURRELL, Q.L. A simple stochastic model for library loans. *Journal of Documentation,* 36(2), June 1980, 115-32.

19. BURRELL, Q.L. Alternative models for library circulation data. *Journal of Documentation,* 38(1), March 1982, 1-13.

20. BURRELL, Q.L. and CANE, V.R. *The analysis of library data.* Manchester: University of Manchester Statistical Laboratory, 1981. (Research Report 83).

21. HINDLE, A. and WORTHINGTON, D. Simple stochastic models for library loans. *Journal of Documentation,* 36(3), September 1980, 209-13.

22. CANE, V.R. A class of non-identifiable stochastic models. *Journal of Applied Probability,* 14(3), 1977, 475-82.

23. FORD, G. *et al. The use of medical literature: a preliminary survey.* London: British Library, 1980. (Research and Development Report No.5515).

24. STUART, I.M. Some effects on library users of the delays in supplying publications. *Aslib Proceedings,* 29(1), January 1977, 35-45.

25. BARR, D. and FARMER, J. Waiting for inter-library loans. *British Library Lending Review,* 5(1), January 1977, 8-12.

26. MORLEY, R. Maximising the benefits from existing library resources. *In: Project for evaluating the benefits from University libraries. Final report.* Durham: University of Durham Computer Unit, 1969. (OSTI Report No.5056).

27. PAYNE, P. *Book selection and use in academic libraries.* London: City of London Polytechnic Library and Learning Resources Services, May 1980. (Library Research Information Sheet).

28. KOHL, D.F. High efficiency inventorying through predictive data. *Journal of Academic Librarianship,* 8(2), May 1982, 82-84.

29. REYNOLDS, L. *Visual presentation of information in COM library catalogues: a survey.* London: British Library, 1979. (Research and Development Report No.5472).

30. SEAL, A. *Full and short entry catalogues: library needs and uses.* Bath: Bath University Library, 1982. (British Library Research and Development Report No.5669).

31. GIFFORD, R. and SOMMER, R. The desk or the bed? *Personnel and guidance journal,* 46(9), 1968, 876-8.

32. SOMMER, R. The ecology of privacy. *Library Quarterly,* 36(3), July 1966, 234-48.

33. SOMMER, R. Reading areas in college libraries. *Library Quarterly*, 38(3), July 1968, 249-60.

34. DEPARTMENT OF EDUCATION AND SCIENCE. *Statistics of Education*, London: HMSO. Vol. 3, 1976. Further Education. Vol.6, 1977. Universities.

DISCUSSION

1. The amount of staff time to be allocated to in-house research was questioned. To what extent should it be continuous? It was thought to be continuous in the sense that any manager should be constantly evaluating his service and many discrete investigations may run consecutively. Whilst Research Librarians are a useful focus for such activity they should not be the sole activists. If this happened other staff would not develop and sustain an appreciation of this management function.

2. The political impact of in-house research was debated. It could work to the political advantage of the library if it can enumerate the need for, and consequences of, action, especially in the area of housekeeping. Many policy decisions are made in academic establishments without any research support. Examples were given of an acceptable cost-beneficial solution to catalogue changes arising out of collaboration with the Centre for Catalogue Research and of the identification of high-use stock using automated circulation records as the basis for joining a cooperative cataloguing network.

3. The problem of investigating the effects of charging were touched on. This was felt to be a topic with strong moral overtones and not an appropriate candidate for experimentation. Moreover, differences between individuals and amongst groups would limit the applicability of one model to a general situation. Thus if charging was introduced as an experiment, many variables would have to be taken into account.

4. With regard to objective-setting and consequent measurement, many situations gave rise almost inadvertently to the defining of objectives. For example, consideration of operational and service issues would raise the question of the library's *raison d'être*. Another approach might arise from the constraints of retrenchment and from research results which indicate, according to the institution and library's response, what the library's function should be. Related measures might be input or output values. The finest arbiters in this area could well be the users. It might be fruitful to ask them to discuss goals and then to constantly refine them.

# NEW PROBLEMS, NEW SOLUTIONS :
# LIBRARY AND INFORMATION TECHNOLOGY

Professor K.G.E. Harris
*Librarian, Newcastle upon Tyne Polytechnic*

I have no intention of defining new technology, because
if you define a thing you then have to justify your definition.
Whatever new technology is, it has come to stay. There are
certain people in the profession who appear to think that if
you hide your head in the sand of a no-redundancy policy the
new technology will go away. An article written by John
Lindsay (1) in a recent issue of *Information and Library
Manager* typifies this attitude. There are other examples of
librarians not wanting to know. A recent meeting of the
Northern Regional Library System Development Sub-Committee
having discussed the future development of libraries and
the second part of the report *The Future Development of
Libraries and Information Services,* commented 'we feel
that too much prominence is given in the report to the
new technology, which is not central to the function
of a library'.

I think that these examples characterise the attitude of
many librarians at the moment and also point to the fact
that staff problems are possibly the key to the whole of the
new technology. The Library Association report (2) about to
be published says that experience in the special library
field seems to show that automation has led to a more efficient
service with fewer staff, and that the jobs most at risk are
those concerned with clerical and more routine operations,
since they are the most easily transferred to an automated
system. This is dubious, even with regard to issue systems,
as most academic libraries are finding that with changes in
educational methods and for other reasons, issues are
increasing to the extent that new technology does not reduce
staff. We had a delightful situation at Newcastle Polytechnic

Library when fines were introduced about a year ago. As a result the total issues increased 25% over one year, and staff issues decreased 17%. This is delightful because it means that staff are returning books more promptly and students are finding the books they need on the shelves. It also means that with a 25% increase in use the issue desk staff cannot be decreased.

As far as types of work are concerned, the opposite of the Library Association's prediction may be true. In cataloguing, clerical operations are becoming much more important, and professional input much less so. A great deal of uncertainty besets discussion of staff costs in relation to the new technology. I suspect that personnel costs are actually going to increase rather than decrease in the long term. In this context, Veaner (3) writes with considerable justice that 'when there is a capacity to perform more work the demand is for more work'. Automated systems are producing increasing amounts of information, some of it useless, which is used for both useful and useless purposes. Further, it may not be true that a considerable advantage of automation is that it can reduce repetitive work. This has, in fact, almost become a cliché. There are certain tasks, such as filing, which have been reduced, but there are plenty of boring jobs remaining which may or may not be connected with automation.

What is true is that there has to be a change in attitude. Librarians and information scientists have to develop new skills and become more like consultants. They are going to offer advice, in many cases they are going to become inter-mediaries, and the function of the librarian as an inter-mediary will be increasingly important. Virtually a new industry will be created for the professional librarian. Abstractors, indexers, people who can manipulate automated systems in the information field, will gain pre-eminence. The corollary of this will be that cataloguers and non-information staff will play a decreasing role and different staff struc-tures will have to be considered. I welcome this change as I have often contended that the more backward the library system the more attention it pays to cataloguing. It may also be necessary to find a completely new role for circulation staff in the light of new developments. Overall there is likely to be a breakdown of traditional professional and non-professional duties, librarians will have to learn a new language because the vocabulary is now becoming more technical and very highly specialised. We are going to be new creatures.

Unfortunately the information technology that has been utilised to date has not particularly changed our attitudes. We still tend to think of information technology as developing further the libraries that we have always had, but this may not be tenable for much longer. Johnson (4) summed the matter up when he wrote 'the on-line catalogue has made the warehouse demonstratively more efficient but it has not changed the passive role it was designed to serve'. In other words, information technology is not going to make librarians more active unless there is a change of attitude. Pauline Atherton (5) gives a beautiful example of the need for new thinking - 'It's hilarious for me to see what university libraries are doing with census data (in the United States). They're creating elaborate cataloguing information about those census tapes instead of providing data services for processing them for the users'. In other words traditional methods are being applied to new technology when they are no longer serving a useful purpose. There is no point in running an eighteenth century library with twentieth century machinery.

Librarians do have an opportunity, if they change their attitude, of becoming much more important, because with the rise of data base searching, and the information explosion, they can become a central element in the information 'business'. At present few other specialists exist in this area, but if librarians do not make themselves indispensable now others will, and indeed are, trying to do so. An information technology working party has been set up at Newcastle Polytechnic. Many departments displayed what to them was a justifiable interest, but few could understand why the library school should want to be represented. This is a cautionary example of how easily opportunities might be lost and how vital the need is for more activity and assertiveness by librarians.

Predicting developments in the field of information technology is fraught with difficulty. Carlson (6), for example, states that information technology is paving the way for an increase in centralised control over economic activity, an increase in representative government and a decrease in personal freedom. Conclusions like this are rife amongst philosophical papers on information technology, but the reasoning behind them is not clear. Papers on the paperless age are interesting but highly speculative. However, a sound and highly recommended article by Richard de Gennaro (7) has recently been published in *Library Journal*.. One or two quotations from this article are very much to the point.

The first states, about information technology, that nothing is impossible to a man who does not have to do it. The second suggests that we are requiring a level of technology which fires the imagination and gives credence to even the most fanciful forecasts. That is equally true. The third asserts that anyone can enjoy the intellectual sport of speculating about the wonders of information technology in the year 2000 and beyond, but some of us must try to see and assess the near term future of that technology and make plans to use it appropriately; and finally, that our experience in the last twenty years should teach us that advances in information technology frequently take longer, cost more, and occur in ways that we do not expect and cannot foresee.

Most of us have to limit our vision when considering information technology. We are not playing games but have to make systems work. As Matthews (8) points out, what the library has to do is first of all identify its present needs, then project them into the future, but possibly not for more than four or five years because beyond that one is reaching the realms of fantasy. Secondly, we have to consider all sorts of alternatives, because using technology is not always the best way of getting things done. In some areas manual operations remain more effective than computerised operations and it is wise to evaluate alternatives very carefully before being committed to futuristic schemes. A recent thesis comparing manual and automated issue systems at Newcastle Polytechnic concluded that the manual system was more cost-effective. The mistake was made in not accounting for a rapidly increasing number of issues which would have soon sabotaged the manual system, quite apart from producing inefficiencies and high cost. This is a salutory lesson which highlights the need for clear thinking when considering exciting technological developments. After all, the end of the book forecast is in the same category as the end of the world forecast. It will happen someday millions of years hence, but the end of the world may come first.

One of the difficulties is that technical improvements appear quite unpredictably. The result is a rash of forecasts; for example, that disc storage is going to be obsolete, video discs, holographic storage and bubble memories will be of primary importance (9). I am sure that a librarian having to plan would love to have a bubble memory, but unfortunately we have to plan with what we actually have. One of the tricks is to try to introduce new systems at a moment which is reasonably appropriate, knowing that there is no such moment. This is one of the great problems. There are so many changes, occurring regularly both in practice and in the development of actual machinery. For instance, there have recently been considerable linkage problems, which are now being resolved. As a result of this a whole new technology has emerged, totally different from the technology of the past. There are no guidelines for planning effectively during such rapid change.

There are certain aspects of new technology which relate to the institutional context of a library. Often new technology is not just a problem for the library but also for the institution which it serves. Consequently the library often finds itself forced into a straight jacket because it has to fit in with an institutional computer policy which has different aims and objectives. At present Newcastle City Libraries are computerising their catalogue - a process largely delimited by the need to process and program the data using the Newcastle City computer. This is an example of a desire to instigate an efficient and useful system which is hampered because the local authority needs to get the maximum use from a computer which is under-used. This sort of problem is one which will affect many library computer developments, since very few libraries are free-standing in this respect. Institutional commitments will always have to be taken into account. There is some truth in Shaughnessy's statement (10) that technology might be a determinant of structure in itself but the changes in technology are also going to be dependent on what happens within your own organisation. He goes on to point out that there is no reason why a twist to this should not take place and that changes in technology themselves can lead to changes in the organisation. This is a possibility which has not been studied carefully. Many examples exist of centralised staff and student records being kept by the institution. These are capable of being applied to a variety of purposes, including library housekeeping. Previously a library would have kept its own records for these purposes. The library is working within an institutional framework which did not exist previously.

There are also new committee structures coming about as a result of the new technology; new computer committees and technology committees with which libraries are having to fit in. New institutional data sources are giving new management possibilities and also new management problems. Following that, there are new relationships within the library; filing

and cataloguing systems are changing, as are many others.
The implications for library buildings and planning are
two-fold. There has to be space for the new machinery, and
in newly designed buildings consideration must be given to
computerised issue systems, public terminals, more flexible
storage, and self-service orientation. Additionally, the
library is actually stocking different types of material,
such as computer programs. The library building needs have
changed as traditional uses change, to the extent that the
library is no longer serving the same purpose. Outside the
organisation new technology will have a profound effect on
national and international library co-ordination. Speaking
about the American scene, Shaugnessy (10) remarks that if
it were not for network and computer technology, would
there really be a National Commission of Libraries and
Information Services in the United States?  Equally if it
were not for the new technology would the impetus for
national co-ordination in this country be so strong?  I
think the answer is that it would not. One of the main planks
in the national co-ordination campaign, despite the attitude
of the Northern Regional Library System, has been the impact
of the new technology. We have to think in terms of modifying
national and international relationships to meet all these
changes, particularly with the internationalisation of
information.

It is possible that a reaction to changes resulting from
new technology will be an increase in resistance to information.
Already the problem of information pollution is being
discussed (11).  It is usual to think in terms of people
who have and always have had a compulsive desire to
publish, and following academic fashions, the back-slapping
habit of mutual quotation and the delight of finding your
name in library catalogues. Information technology will
bolster this activity. The result will be, as Mignon (12)
points out, that as the information explosion increases,
society become more antipathetic towards information. Already
professional people in all sorts of areas are being drowned
in memos and reports, surveys and lists. Librarians are
helping to encourage this, when really we have a vested
interest in seeing that the flow of information is restricted
somewhat, not only for our own sanity, but also so that it
might be more useful. Nevertheless, although the information
explosion came before the information technology explosion,
the two are now definitely going hand in hand. One can see
that this plethora can lead to a reaction, and in some

respects the sooner the better. Part of the trouble, as Aines (13) says, is that we have fallen in love with information technology, and certainly with the tools, so that we persist as librarians in creating all sorts of information systems even when the users are not asking for them. The result is many databases of minimal use to parallel many libraries of minimal use.

Librarians should be thinking now of how to harness information technology in order to combat the information overload which we are now all faced with. The information explosion and Information Technology Year has to some extent led to new thinking on libraries as libraries. It is possibly an exaggeration to claim, as Johnson (4) does, that the natural repository for electronic information is not in the library but in the computer. This is a doubtful proposition, and especially so if the library becomes a service area and not a dump for unwanted material. It will then remain the natural depository for information.

Nevertheless the growth of home information services have to be taken into account. This has not begun very auspiciously. Prestel, Gateway and its successors have not been marketed properly. They are growing, however, and should prompt librarians to consider how they can become service agents to information, feeding Prestel and becoming more involved in community information.

At the same time the information centre, which is the library if it is a proper library, is going to remain absolutely central for major information enquiries. We have failed to realise in the past, but must recognise now, that the computer has actually allowed libraries to take on a more significant role whilst changing the whole information environment. Johnson (4) for example, and many others, are clear that libraries have to develop expertise as switching centres for electronic information. The concept of the library as a document delivery centre could be the key to their survival in the new technological age, and it is these areas upon which future plans must be based. De Gennaro (7) states that the bibliographic search function has been successfully computerised, although I would doubt that to some extent, and adds that the document delivery function has not. This is broadly true, and it is an area which possibly receives too little attention. The document delivery services which have been developed, like LEXIS and NEXIS, are rather crude and not particularly effective. They are the forerunners of things to come, and they will eventually become much more effective and much less expensive, provided that their development is properly planned.

De Gennaro (7) offers comfort when he says that most of the new technology-based businesses are still largely dependent on the library market for survival, and that the new information brokers ultimately rely on libraries as the source for most of the documents which they supply to their clients. I would endorse this claim enthusiastically. Libraries will always function as the providers of basic bibliographical information, or whatever information is required. This role cannot be easily eroded.

Concerning the technological aspects of information technology, far too many librarians have made themselves into little mechanics, and that is not really a function of the librarian. There are three technical areas, however, that are interesting. These are data transmission technology, computer technology, and image storage and display technology (12). All of these have a part to play and are areas where librarians ought to develop some sort of interest, at the same time keeping their hands reasonably clean. New technology can bring many technical problems of, for example, maintenance, repair, system reliability, and the need for back-up systems. In addition one must consider response time, limitation of terminals, the quality of the data bases, and special networking problems. Indeed, there are very serious problems at the moment with the actual technology. It does not always provide what is needed because the machinery has not yet been perfected. Matthews (8) outlines a progression which reflects the experiences of many. He describes the life cycle of an automated integrated library system which starts off with wild euphoria, followed by growing concern, followed by near total disillusionment, followed by unmitigated disaster, followed finally by the search for the guilty. It is also true that the development of some of our complex systems has frequently been completely out of proportion to the results achieved.

There are now new possibilities with microcomputers. This is an important development because, as Williams (14) states, the early computerised library systems depended in practically all cases on an existing main-frame which was somewhere in the institution, and/or bureau services, and did not give libraries sufficient control over their operations. Often the major problem was that libraries had no control over computer staff, so that batch processing systems were unsatisfactory and did not help library operations at all. Difficulties were also created because the computer unit or department dictated what sort of system the library would have. With the development of mini-computer systems the library can have much more control over what it actually wants and what it gets. The power of the computer staff, as Swanson (15) points out, is like that of the grand inquisitor which comes to be based on miracle, mystery and authority. That mystery is disappearing. With the new generation of systems, including off-the-shelf systems like GEAC, the library can have much greater control over its own information technology systems. The micro-computer could be the salvation of library technology, and solve many of the problems of the past.

Co-operation is an area which, as yet, has not been properly studied in relation to information technology. I think that the possibilities are tremendous and extend well beyond cataloguing networks, but require a positive commitment to thinking co-operatively which does not preclude a critical approach. In a letter recently published in the *Library Association Record* (16) I suggest that what we need now after the self-renewing library, especially with regard to networked data bases, is the self-renewing catalogue. One of the great dangers of the data bases we are creating for catalogue purposes is that they are becoming large and unwieldy and difficult to use. What we really require now are streamlined data bases for initial use with a back-up system, in the same way that the self-renewing library depends on the British Library back-up system. Without the British Library there would be no self-renewing library philosophy. This is the sort of thinking which is needed for planning the co-operative use of automated systems. One can see the dangers already with OCLC which, I suspect, is now becoming far too massive, and where response times are becoming highly critical.

Finally, with regard to research - the Library Association report (2) suggests three areas in which research ought to be undertaken. The first is that those technological developments of most use must be identified; in other words research has to be realistic. Secondly, work already undertaken in special areas such as document delivery, resource sharing, data base design, and the physical design of libraries, should be developed. These are all areas which are very important and which urgently require investigation. The third is equally important; the management of change in users' attitudes and requirements.

I will finish with another quotation from De Gennaro (7), in which he refers to the paperless society: 'in that society not only libraries but the institutions and the scholars they serve may also become obsolete'. We cannot do much now to prepare for that kind of massive change, so if libraries go down as a result of the new technology, we know at least that universities and polytechnics will go down with them.

REFERENCES

1.  LINDSAY, J. Last stand at Thermopylae, or the onward march of the space invaders. *Information and library manager*, 2(1), June 1982, 12-13.

2.  LIBRARY ASSOCIATION. *Report on the impact of new technology on libraries and information centres.* London: Library Association, 1982.

3.  VEANER, A.B. Management and technology. *IFLA Journal*, 7(1), 1981, 32-37.

4.  JOHNSON, M.F. After the online catalog. *American Libraries*, 13(4), April 1982, 235-9.

5.  ATHERTON, P.A. Comments on papers of Dr Carl Hammer and Prof. P.A. Atherton. *In:* Chartrand, R.L. and Morenz, J.W. *(eds). Information technology serving society.* London: Pergamon Press, 1979, p.51.

6.  CARLSON, J.W. Where information technology is taking us. *In:* Chartrand, R.L. and Morenz, J.W. *(eds). Information technology serving society.* London: Pergamon Press, 1979, pp.113-17.

7.  De GENNARO, R. Libraries, technology and the information market place. *Library journal*, 107(11), 1 June 1982, 1045-54.

8.  MATTHEWS, J.R. 20 Qs and As on automated integrated library systems. *American libraries*, 13(6), June 1982, 367-71.

9.  LUNDEEN, G. The role of microcomputers in libraries. *Wilson Library Bulletin*, 55(3), November 1980, 178-85.

10. SHAUGHNESSY, T.W. Technology and the structure of libraries. *Libri,* 32(2), June 1982, 149-55.

11. MADDOCK, Sir I. Is the information environment being polluted? *In:* Taylor, P.J. *(ed). New trends in documentation and information: proceedings of the 39th FID Congress, University of Edinburgh, 25-28 September 1978.* London: Aslib, 1980, pp.13-16.

12. MIGNON, E. Telecommunications and the research library: a partisan overview. *Information services and use,* 1(4), January 1982, 207-14.

13. AINES, A.A. Comment *In:* Chartrand, R.L. and Morenz, J.W. *(eds). Information technology serving society.* London: Pergamon Press, 1979, pp.52-3.

14. WILLIAMS, P.W. and GOLDSMITH, G. Information retrieval on mini- and micro-computers. *In:* Williams, M.E. *(ed). Annual review of information science and technology,* Volume 16, 1981. New York: Knowledge Industry Publications Inc., 1981, pp. 85-111.

15. SWANSON, D.R. Miracles, microcomputers and librarians. *Library Journal,* 107(11), 1 June 1982, 1055-59.

16. HARRIS, K.G.E. Rapid access catalogues. (Letter). *Library Association Record,* 84(7/8), July/August 1982, 253.

DISCUSSION

1.  Some debate took place about the continued precedence of cataloguing as a use for computerisation. Even acknowledging the need for detailed subject cataloguing of computer programs, it was predicted that developments in information technology would show other emphases.

2.  The concept of a self-renewing data base was described and debated. It was allied to the idea of the self-renewing library, and exemplified to some extent by SCOLCAP. In this instance the most-used records are identified, less-used items forming a back-up resource. Initial searches therefore exploit a streamlined data base more rapidly than a continually growing record such as that being developed by OCLC. It was felt that this principle would hold even if technological developments greatly increased search times and on-line access to readers became more widespread.

3.  With regard to the growing use of microprocessors and Local Area Networks, it was felt that more libraries would use self-contained systems for housekeeping and information processing. If this were so, regional networks as they now functioned would become redundant. External and national data bases might then support local resources by providing fuller references than those used internally, which would be simplified.

4.  The effects of new technology on employment were considered, and it was felt that opportunities existed and should be sought positively. This applied to librarians and others displaced by its advent. Librarians had relevant education and experience and could become information brokers, selecting, inputting and retrieving information. An additional role would be that of user education, teaching retrieval techniques.

    The academic role of the librarian was seen as being increasingly important. Technical services activities, formerly classed as professional, should be reviewed and professional energies directed towards the interpretation and provision of information. In filling this role librarians must be aware of other services and facilities to which they might relate, and not take a blinkered approach which could isolate them from the mainstream of developments.

# NEW PROBLEMS, NEW SOLUTIONS :
# CO-OPERATION AND RESOURCE SHARING

Malcolm Smith
*Head of Monographic Records, British Library Lending Division*

In this paper I propose to look particularly at the current very intense activity which aims to establish a new framework for interlending and other co-operative activities. In particular:

a)  the work of the newly revamped Library and Information Services Council (LISC), particularly its report, *The future development of libraries and information services.2.Working together within a national framework* (1).

b)  the soon-to-be published report of the British Library Ad Hoc Working Party on Union Catalogues (2), whose recommendations are appended.

c)  the work of the Co-operative Automation Group, which is providing a channel for communication between the British Library and the library automation co-operatives.

I hope to look at what these three groups are saying and examine whether we are witnessing the demise of library co-operation as we have experienced it over the past fifty years, and its possible replacement by co-ordinated activities which are much more purposeful and directed.

## LIBRARY AND INFORMATION SERVICES COUNCIL

The report of the Library and Information Services Council *Working together within a national framework* makes a suitable starting point for examining our subject. Its very title illustrates the difference in approach from the voluntary

non-paying co-operation between libraries which has tended
to be dominant in the past. The report examines some of the
'major influences on the future development of library and
information services and some of the resulting problems'. It
looks to the Office of Arts and Libraries to 'influence
events and encourage action by promoting discussion' and by
issuing guidelines.

The report makes a distinction between a 'holdings'
strategy and an 'access' strategy. Developments in communications, the information explosion - which may have abated for
the time being - the growth in automated services, and
perhaps most markedly, the financial pressures of the
recession, have all contributed to the difficulty of
sustaining the traditional approach. This regards the library
as a storehouse of knowledge which aims to satisfy its
objectives largely from its own resources. This is the
approach the report describes as the 'holdings' strategy.
The report argues that the 'access' strategy recognises the
need ' to develop more effective means of drawing upon the
library and information resources of the country as a whole
to supplement, or even replace, their own resources', and
that this should have a major place in policy formulation.

This need is most vividly illustrated in the growth of
new possibilities for the production and dissemination of
information. In particular, developments in video discs and
their use to support full-text information retrieval systems
may have a big impact on the role of each individual library.
It is too early to state with any certainty the shape which such
new technology will take. We may see centrally-held stores
of information on video discs linked to users by conventional
transport/postal links, or at a later stage, by reliable
facsimile transmission perhaps using satellites for
communication over long distances. On the other hand,
developments may take the form of distributed installations
of video disc storage and retrieval devices which will enable
a library to hold its own materials in an entirely new way.
Much depends on the progress of projects such as ADONIS
which is funded by a consortium of the major scientific
journal publishers including Elsevier Science Publishers, and
the European Community's ambitious ARTEMIS concept. As you
may know the British Library has been holding discussions
with the ADONIS consortium but it is by no means clear yet
as to what, if any, form of involvement may emerge. However,

there is clearly scope for research into the relationships
between libraries, publishers, booksellers and telecommunica-
tion providers, to ensure that what emerges from this period
of rapid technological development meets the needs of users.
Indeed the Library and Information Services Council recommends
that formal arrangements should be set up whereby they and
the Office of Arts and Libraries review the progress and
application of new technology.

One important point made in the report is that 'many
libraries are capable of adopting wider objectives if their
institutions allow them to do so and if suitable financial
provision can be made'. This is particularly relevant where
the financial provision is from the same source. For example,
a local authority may be funding college, school, public and
polytechnic libraries in close proximity to each other.
Philip Sewell's survey of *Library Co-operation in the United
Kingdom* (3) devotes a chapter to what he calls local modular
schemes of co-operation. These involve libraries of different
types in a particular area meeting together to improve links
and co-ordinate specialist activities to avoid duplication of
effort, or perhaps, as the only means of ensuring that certain
services get off the ground. The objectives and achievements
of the groupings which exist are worthy of examination,
particularly in terms of their costs and benefits, in order
to improve our understanding of the scope for this form of
co-operation.

One of the points exercising the Library and Information
Services Council in their report was the need for another
review of the regional library systems of this country. A
substantial annex sets out what they regard as the relevant
issues. The systems themselves, through the National Committee
on Regional Library Co-operation, looked at their role five
years ago, partly in response to an examination of the
relative costs and effectiveness of borrowing from the
British Library Lending Division (BLLD) compared with pro-
ceeding through the regional systems. This study, which
involved the West Midlands Regional Library System (4),
illustrated that, at least where the Lending Division is
able to supply an item from its own stock, it is likely to
cost less than using the regional library system and to be as
effective in terms of satisfaction rate and supply time. I
have just completed the first draft of a report on a further
exercise looking at the total costs of interlending which

involved a variety of different types of libraries. I am therefore particularly conscious at the moment of the immense practical difficulties of comparing costs between different institutions, as those of you will be who have been involved in the recent work of the Centre for Interfirm Comparison which examines the costs of academic and public libraries (5). However, the figures from this recent study also indicate that interlending requests which involve the regional library systems are more expensive than those which do not.

It is therefore perhaps surprising that LISC feels that greater benefits may be obtained from the regional systems as each introduces or expands its automation. Nevertheless they are right to emphasize that at present the regional library systems complement, rather than compete with, the services of BLLD, particularly since the 1977 review which identified the strengths of each party. From the academic library's point of view the main value of the regional library system, apart perhaps from the transport schemes in the areas in which they operate, may well be as a source of additional locations of recent monographs which are not immediately available from BLLD. There is no certainty, however, that the often recently published, much-requested items at Boston Spa are available for interlending from other libraries. It may be that this is an area which could be investigated further, although I would resist any suggestion that members of regional library systems revert to co-operative acquisition programmes to provide a better coverage for interlibrary loans. Arrangements such as the inter-regional subject specialization schemes were never an entirely satisfactory source for the demands of academic libraries, and financial stringencies will probably ensure that any reintroduction of this concept would be short-lived.

In a related American context, I was interested to read the comments of Ballard in an article contained in a recent issue of *Library Journal* entitled *Public library networking: neat, plausible, wrong* (6). He says:

'Public librarians are only behaving logically when they abandon resource sharing activities at the first sign of financial distress. It is truly a marginal activity. The very fact that librarians, having experience...with systems, refuse to contribute local monies for their continuance should be the best possible indicator of their value (or lack thereof).'

I feel that the case for centralized funding for the provision of extra copies of titles in demand at the Lending Division is stronger than the case for additional funds for the rebirth of subject specialization schemes. These schemes are an example of the old-style voluntary co-operation which I have already contrasted with the co-ordinated approach to resources which is now emerging.

A final point with regard to the LISC report is that it notes the extent to which the whole library network is now dependent on the British Library's co-ordinating role. This is also brought out in the rather dire wording of a paragraph in the Councils 1980/81 review of library and information services (7):

'We draw attention to the extent to which libraries have become dependent on facilities provided centrally by the British Library, and especially by the British Library Lending Division. Local and other services have been developed to draw upon and to complement those available from this source, and withdrawal or serious reduction of the British Library's service would have disastrous effects throughout the country. In this situation there are bound to be fears at any threat to its financial support. We urge therefore that no such change should be contemplated without the fullest consultation with all relevant interests, including the Library and Information Services Council.'

BRITISH LIBRARY AD HOC WORKING PARTY ON UNION CATALOGUES

It is on this warning note that I turn our attention more specifically to interlending, and the report of the British Library Ad Hoc Working Party on Union Catalogues. This will shortly be available from the British Library as a *gratis* publication and it is hoped that it will be widely read and discussed. It represents the deliberations of a dozen representatives of the British Library, the Library Association, the Standing Conference of National and University Librarians (SCONUL), The Council of Polytechnic Librarians (COPOL) and the regional library systems, over the past eighteen months.

I would like to concentrate particularly on those recommendations which illustrate the trends and problems caused in the field of interlending by the introduction of computers into areas such as acquisitions and circulation control. The manner in which automation has an effect beyond the activities directly affected by it is a good example of why co-ordination and investigation is needed over a much broader front than in the past. For instance, the impact of newer technologies such as video discs should be thoroughly examined so that the effects on the user are clearly understood before major decisions are taken.

The particular concern of the Working Party, which restricts itself to considering the interlending of monographs, was the possibility of a shift away from the highly centralized interlending arrangements that now operate in this country, towards the smaller networks of libraries who share computer facilities, particularly those who are members of the library co-operatives. This shift, while not consciously planned, was likely to come about for a number of reasons. One of these is the Lending Division's increasing reliance on recovering its costs from user libraries, which gives the impression to borrowers that its services are becoming expensive. Another is the attraction of knowing positively, through a union catalogue on fiche or through access on-line to another library's holdings, that a particular title required on interlibrary loan has been acquired by an identified library. This attraction increases in those situations where member libraries could ascertain whether the item required was currently available for loan by access to the circulation files of the holding library. However, the dangers of this development also need to be considered. The members of co-operatives are no more geared to cope primarily with inter-library loans than any other libraries in this country, with the single exception of the British Library Lending Division. They comprise libraries with major holdings as well as those with more limited stocks, and the pressure on the former if they become large net lenders may well become intolerable. As in the United States, we might well see the imposition of additional charges, perhaps set at a punitive level, to discourage this activity. Although this may result in a return to centralized interlending based on the Lending Division, the damage done in the meantime to the Division's finances and to the service it could provide might prove irreversible.

The Working Party has recognized that it is neither sensible
nor desirable to attempt to assess the activities of library
co-operatives solely on the grounds that the pattern of interlending might be affected. However, its report does make the
consequences of such developments clear and, it is hoped, will
lead to a wider understanding of the problem. Similarly, the
Lending Division hopes that the total costs of interlending
transactions will be more widely appreciated if it proves
possible to publish the results of the current investigations
into costs. The basis of the Working Party's approach has
therefore been to ensure that the Lending Division is able
to compete on level terms with libraries within the
co-operatives. It has not adopted the line that all interlending for monographs should be channelled through the
Division; instead it prefers to provide a system which will
ensure that the central stock of higher level English language
books from the developed world, which are in heavy demand,
is exploited to the full. Different arrangements, relying
either on automated union catalogues as in the case of other
Western European language monographs, or on informed specula-
tion, for example in the field of Asian monographs, are
proposed.

Thus the Working Party's report proposes that the Lending
Division should create a machine-readable file of records of
its monograph stock which should be made widely available
as a Computer Output Microform (COM) catalogue, on-line and
in ISBN form, as part of the existing Combined Regional
Locations List. This recommendation is already being acted
upon by the Lending Division and a specification of the
computer requirements is likely to go out to tender later
this year. This development is an interesting example of
automation being introduced not primarily as a cost-saving
exercise, but to enhance service. Indeed, because the Lending
Division's existing cataloguing procedures are particularly
basic, cataloguing to a standard which would be compatible
with other machine-readable files of records may be more
intensive of resources. The Division is also taking the
opportunity to automate its acquisitions procedures at the
same time, as part of an integrated system. It is hoped that
it will be possible to operate an automated system from the
beginning of 1984 and a limited retrospective conversion of
stock records is being contemplated, perhaps back to 1980.
In order to assist our users, the dividing line between the
automated and manual systems will probably be by publication
date, although this will mean that the union catalogue cannot
be closed.

The Working Party proposes that this widely available automated stock catalogue is supplemented by a machine readable Union Finding List of Foreign Language Monographs. This should also be available to potential borrowers in COM form, and possibly on-line. The intention is to maintain coverage of libraries' holdings at least at the present level of the existing union catalogue of books. There may well be some alterations to the list of contributing libraries to favour those who are able to supply notifications of additions and withdrawals in machine readable form. Nevertheless the most valuable collections must continue to be incorporated in the new list, even where only manual notifications are available. The widespread availability of this finding list will encourage libraries to engage in direct interlending of foreign language monographs, and may have consequences for the amount of such material acquired by the Division. However, demand in this area is widely scattered over a very broad range of titles and the Lending Division already frequently relies on other libraries to supply this material. Again, this recommendation is being actively pursued by the Lending Division as part of its monograph automation project, and it is the intention that for internal purposes foreign language notifications will be part of a single integrated database which will include the English language stock records.

Thus, if the finances are available, there is a good chance that within a few years the interlibrary loan department of a borrowing library will have a record on fiche of the holdings of recent publications held at the Lending Division, and of other libraries' foreign language acquisitions. The proposed addition of the ISBNs of the Lending Division stock to the currently available regional or combined listings of locations will also have a considerable impact on the way this tool is used. At present it is not possible to predict whether there will be a generally available combined listing of British Library Lending Division and all regional holdings or whether the Lending Division's holdings will be added separately to each of the existing regional files. As the Working Party report notes, this is a matter for discussion within the National Committee on Regional Library Co-operation.

The total impact of the availability of these new inter-lending tools may be considerable and should be studied with some care. Fortunately, the Library and Information Services Council has prepared a list of questions which it feels are relevant to the consideration of new co-operative and

co-ordinating arrangements. These are published as an annex
to the report *Working together within a national framework*
(1), and is to be hoped that the library community will
satisfy itself that the proposed arrangements meet the
following criteria:

1.  *Does the scheme add to the effectiveness of the
    information services of the country as a whole?*

    I have attempted to give enough of the background
    to the study to indicate why I believe it does.

2.  *Do the objectives of the scheme conflict with those
    of any other?*

    There was the danger that conflict could arise
    between the proponents of centralized interlending
    and those prepared to see direct lending predominate.
    However it is hoped that the report has provided a
    solution which is acceptable to all parties. This
    should be evident during the next few months as the
    library community reacts to the report.

3.  *Does the scheme allow something which is needed, to
    be done which previously was not done or was not
    done so well?*

    The new arrangements fall firmly into the latter
    category.

4.  *Will the scheme provide to as many users as high a
    standard of service as is already being given?*

    The standard of service should be higher because the
    recommendations of the report will not lead to the
    removal of any existing facilities but provide
    additional ones.

5.  *Will the scheme enable savings to be made whilst
    providing as good or better service than before?
    If not, is it cost-effective?*

    This is a difficult question to answer just now, but
    it is important that the report's recommendations are
    viewed from this angle.

6. *Does the scheme have the financial, technological and staff resources to achieve its objectives in the most effective manner? In particular, does it take sufficient account of new technology?*

The question of resources is particularly crucial. In the present situation it would be foolish for anyone to state unequivocally that the resources needed for the efficient implementation of all the recommendations will be available. The report itself makes it clear that much depends on resources becoming available, but it is hoped that a tangible start can be made within the next two years. While the report is very much concerned with the repercussions of new technology, it has not been able to go into much detail about the implications of on-line access, as opposed to access through COM. This is an area which will be touched on later.

7. *Is the constitution of the scheme soundly based and so structured that it is capable of adaptation or improvement?*

The Working Party which was responsible for the report was fully aware of the need to take into account other factors which could affect the pattern of interlending, and although it has now disbanded, the developments which it envisages will be reviewed by the Lending Division's Advisory Committee.


CO-OPERATIVE AUTOMATION GROUP

This group, set up by the British Library, has amongst its members representatives of the UK library co-operatives - BLAISE/LOCAS, BLCMP, LASER, SCOLCAP and SWALCAP.* A brief

---

| * | BLAISE/LOCAS | British Library Automated Information Service/ Local Catalogue Service |
| | BLCMP | Birmingham Libraries Co-operative Mechanisation Project |
| | LASER | London and South Eastern Library Region |
| | SCOLCAP | Scottish Libraries Co-operative Automation Project |
| | SWALCAP | South West Academic Libraries Co-operative Automation Project |

description of the functions of these services and of the
Co-operative Automation Group (CAG) appears in an article
in a recent issue of *Aslib Proceedings* (8). The Group was
formed to try to ensure that there was the necessary degree
of co-ordination between the services provided by the co-
operatives and the national library, and was partly inspired
by the comments of the Select Committee on Education, Science
and Arts (9).

   The co-operatives, with the exception of LASER which has a
rather different history in that is is primarily an interlending organisation, were the product of a desire to utilise
the resources of the computer, particularly for cataloguing,
at a time when only the very largest of libraries could afford
to have a dedicated machine of their own and to employ the
expertise required to construct their own systems. Despite
the dramatic reduction in the costs of computing equipment,
the co-operatives have continued to expand both in numbers
of customers and in the breadth of their services, largely
because there has been no corresponding reduction in the
costs of software and systems design. The addition of
acquisitions and circulation control functions to the original
cataloguing service, together with the implications for
interlending in the emergence of new union catalogues, have
resulted in a wide range of services being made available to
prospective customers.

   It should be remembered that this growth is taking place
at the same time as the British Library is providing a similar
service for cataloguing and also for information retrieval
through its BLAISE/LOCAS service. Indeed, all the co-operatives
either mount on their own databases, or have permanent links
with, the database of UK MARC records created by the British
Library for the national bibliography. Nevertheless, there is
a considerable amount of  cataloguing carried on by all the
organisations represented on CAG of Extra Marc Material (EMMA).
The total number of EMMA records held on the co-operatives
probably exceeds the approximately two million UK and LC MARC
records now available. Although there will obviously be
overlap between the various files of EMMA records, the extent
of this is not known. The result is that many items are being
catalogued more than once to produce similar MARC type records
on co-operative databases. There would appear to be *prima facie*
case for some co-ordination in this area and an investigation
into the practicability of a national database. However, the
implications of such a development go beyond the elimination
of unnecessary duplication of cataloguing effort.

Firstly there is the vexed question of standards. We have made much progress over the past fifteen years with the introduction of MARC formats and more recently with AACR2. Perhaps the former will provide the flexibility required to ensure the general acceptance of a national cataloguing standard. Secondly, how can any national database be exploited beyond its use as a vast store of cataloguing data? It might perhaps become a widely-used potential requirements file to be used in automated acquisition systems or for bibliographic checking. It may have a beneficial effect on the timeliness of the appearance of MARC records for newly published books, and perhaps take some of the pressure off the Bibliographic Services Division of the British Library. A database of this sort could include holdings information and become a formidable interlending tool. Thus it is interesting to note that there is now a representative of the British Library Lending Division on CAG, who has acted as a link with the Ad Hoc Working Party on Union Catalogues. Obviously, the usefulness of the machine-readable record of Lending Division stock would be enhanced if it were to be incorporated into the holdings information available on a national database, particularly as the Division is now equipped to receive requests by computer links.

This is not by any means an exhaustive list of the implications which a national data-base might have but it should serve to provoke some thought and discussion. It must be clear that we are facing a period of quite intense activity. It will be different in character from the voluntary co-operation which has developed in various directions over the past fifty years. Undoubtedly the atmosphere of retrenchment has accelerated this process. The general thrust of the Library and Information Services Council, and the Office of Arts and Libraries, is towards the provision of a co-ordinated network, and the shape of this will soon be clearly discernable. The report of the Ad Hoc Working Party on Union Catalogues provides many of the pointers, and the work of the Co-operative Automation Group will provide some more. The time is now ripe for a constructive discussion on the wide range of implications of these developments.

REFERENCES

1.  DEPARTMENT OF EDUCATION AND SCIENCE OFFICE OF ARTS
    AND LIBRARIES. *The future development of libraries and
    information services*. London: HMSO, 1982. (Library
    Information Series No.12).

2.  *The report of the British Library Ad Hoc Working Party
    on Union Catalogues*. London: British Library, 1982.

3.  SEWELL, P.H. *Library co-operation in the United Kingdom*.
    London: British Library, 1979. (Research and Development
    Report No.5479).

4.  SMITH, M.D. *A comparative study of the inter-library
    lending services provided by the West Regional Library
    System and the British Library Lending Division*.
    London: British Library, 1977. (Research and Development
    Report No.5319).

5.  CENTRE FOR INTERFIRM COMPARISON. *Inter-library comparisons:
    pilot comparison with public libraries*. London: British
    Library, 1981. (Research and Development Report No.5638).

6.  BALLARD, T. Public library networking: neat, plausible,
    wrong. *Library Journal*, 107(7), April 1, 1982, 679-683.

7.  DEPARTMENT OF EDUCATION AND SCIENCE. *Report by the
    Minister for the Arts on library and information
    matters during 1981*. London: HMSO, 1981. (Cmnd. 8454).

8.  BAKEWELL, K.G.B. The UK library networks and the
    Co-operative Automation Group. *Aslib Proceedings*,
    34(6/7), June/July 1982, 301-309.

9.  EDUCATION, SCIENCE AND ARTS COMMITTEE (HOUSE OF COMMONS).
    *Information storage and retrieval in the British
    Library service*. London: HMSO, 1980. (Reports 1979-80.
    HC 767, 409 i-iv).

APPENDIX

From:  REPORT OF THE BRITISH LIBRARY AD HOC WORKING PARTY
       ON UNION CATALOGUES


RECOMMENDATIONS

These recommendations have been formulated with due regard
to the need to contain spending within reasonable limits.
Whilst some require detailed systems work to be done before
the true costs are established, the Working Party considers
that these proposals constitute the minimum requirement to
maintain an effective and efficient interlending system for
the future. Therefore the Working Party earnestly hopes
that the British Library will make available the necessary
resources.

1.   The Lending Division should create a machine-readable
     file of records of its English and foreign language
     monograph stock, which should then be made available
     as a COM catalogue, on-line and in ISBN form as part
     of the Combined Regional Locations List. (Sections 5.1
     and 5.2).

2.   This file should initially contain records for items
     published after the date of its inception, and as
     much of pre-existing stock as is feasible. To simplify
     use the dividing line between old and new catalogue
     files should be drawn by date of publication. (Section 5.1).

3.   When Lending Division stock appears in the Combined
     Regional Locations List, the possibility of distributing
     it to individual regional members and other libraries
     should be pursued. (Section 5.2).

4.   The Lending Division should create a machine-readable
     Union Finding List of Foreign Language Monographs, which
     would be made available in COM form and possibly on-line.
     Libraries should be encouraged to use this finding list
     to locate items for interlibrary access. (Section 5.3).

5.   The Union Finding List of Foreign Language Monographs
     should endeavour to maintain at least as good a level
     of coverage of material as the present Union Catalogue
     of Books. To this end it may be necessary to retain
     some non-automated contributors, such as the smaller
     specialist libraries. (Section 5.3.)

6.    The Lending Division should investigate the possibility
      of adding records retrospectively to the Union Finding
      List of Foreign Language Monographs, where they are
      available in machine-readable form. As with the Lending
      Division stock catalogue the dividing line between the
      Union Finding List and the Union Catalogue of Books
      should be by date of publication. (Section 5.3).

7.    The record structure adopted for the Lending Division
      stock catalogue and the Union Finding List of Foreign
      Language Monographs should be MARC compatible, but the
      content need be no more than is required for inter-
      library access. (Section 7).

8.    It is recommended that work should commence as soon
      as possible on development of the proposed stock and
      union catalogues and on the internal systems required
      to build and exploit them at the Lending Division
      (Section 8).

9.    The implementation of these recommendations should be
      kept under close review. The Lending Division Advisory
      Committee is felt to be the most appropriate body, and
      it has agreed to accept this role. (Section 5.5).

DISCUSSION

1.  Most of the discussion centred on the question of the
    National Data Base, its cost and usefulness, and on its
    relationship to the data bases of co-operative systems.

    It was explained that the intention was to make
    information on the BLLD's holdings more widely available,
    and to aid those libraries whose holdings were generally
    known but could not sustain large inter-loan demands.
    With regard to the data bases of co-operative systems,
    it was not thought technically feasible to interrogate
    them sequentially and that access to a national data
    base would be more efficient. An exception to this
    concept will probably be made with regard to foreign
    language material. In this instance it would be in the
    interests of the BLLD and other libraries to build up
    a stock amongst certain libraries as a national resource.

2.  With reference to the recent comparative costing of the
    various interloan systems undertaken by the BLLD, notice
    was taken of the hidden costs and variables likely to
    affect direct interlending and use of the regional
    systems. The costing exercise had been intended partially
    to illustrate that direct interlending did involve
    substantial hidden costs. These should be considered
    when comparing the immediate cost of using the Lending
    Divisions resources. Factors affecting costs of involve-
    ment in regional schemes include the extent of demand
    on one's own stock and the efficacy of a transport
    scheme. With regard to the cost per item borrowed as
    against its acquisition, although borrowing appears to
    be cheaper, this might be altered if a relevance factor
    was added to the transaction. Studies have shown that if
    abstracts of potential interloan items are available,
    demand is reduced.

# THE FUTURE : THE LIBRARIAN
# AS MANAGER

Ian Rogerson
*Librarian, Manchester Polytechnic*

This paper does not seek to illustrate detailed management techniques employed within a Polytechnic Library in times of retrenchment. Those interested in the Manchester experience are referred to the paper given at the Library Association University, College and Research Section Annual Conference of 1981 (1). Rather it seeks to identify the nature, history and possible duration of the cuts in library expenditure, particularly in the public sector of higher education in the United Kingdom.

The fact that many librarians have found few friends in defending libraries from cuts in public expenditure should come as no surprise. There have been, and always will be, enemies of books, including those whom Lord Goodman accuses of using poisonous arguments to suggest that there are too many libraries (2). Those responsible for running our public libraries have in the last 15 years to a large extent discounted their historic creed of education, information and recreation, replacing this with a synonym for the last, i.e. leisure. Education is a function for which most public libraries have ceased to cater presumably because of the growth of academic libraries. Information provision now appears to be concentrated on community information, with community having a strange semantic connotation. The emphasis on leisure was a conscious, though naive, decision taken as a result of the forecast of a leisure society which would come about in the closing decades of the twentieth century, and which presumably would have to be catered for with the inevitable consequence of increased funding. That forecast has become true with hideous consequences. There is now a figure in excess of 3 million unemployed. This figure is unlikely to come down in the near future, and what have the

public libraries gained in resources to cope with this new
leisured class? Nothing but front-line casualties in each
successive round of cuts. Presumably the money saved as a
result goes out in the form of social security benefits to
feed the bellies and not the minds of this new leisured
class. It is likely that many will die earlier as a direct
or indirect result of unemployment, and those librarians who
work in Departments of Leisure Services will find their
colleagues in Parks and Cemeteries receiving an increased
share of the departmental revenue at the expense of the
library. This view of the current British public library
scene is not irrelevant to the subject of your conference.
The point made here is that public libraries are not essential.
The disposal of the dead is inescapable. Thus, there are no
votes in libraries.

There are no votes in academic libraries. At present this
is being demonstrated in a number of institutions where
teaching and non-teaching jobs are being protected by library
cuts. Whilst there are those such as Professor Kemp, who in a
recent letter to *The Guardian* (3) protested about the proposed
sale of part of Glasgow University's inheritance to help
ensure the institution's survival, there are others, for
example Dr Judith Hook, who in a subsequent letter (4) pro-
claimed that she would rather leave her personal library to
an institution which values its people above its property.
In this kind of debate librarians seem particularly lacking
in the knowledge and use of the fundamental arguments.

Turning to the *Concise Oxford English Dictionary*, its
first definition of the word 'library' is a room or building
containing books for reading or reference. During the mid-
1950s when an upsurge of technical college building was
taking place, I was appointed to create a library in one of
those colleges. Its Principal constantly invaded the new
library with a procession of visitors proudly announcing in
a loud voice on each occasion that 'This is the library
where the books are kept.' Twenty-five years later I am
still conscious that those in power in the public sector of
higher education are those least dependent upon the library
for their academic sustenance.

To obtain a true definition of what a library is, and
more particularly an academic or scholarly library, the
writings of Raymond Irwin (5) are helpful. Irwin uses an

analogy of the golden chain of the Athenian Academy, in this
case the golden chain of written record as the conquerer of
space and time. Libraries are the strands interwoven in the
chain, communities 'in which both reader and writer meet, to
which both contribute something of value, mutually forging
the links of the chain as it passes from mind to mind and
from generation to generation'(6). Irwin maintains that the
Librarian 'has two main duties...(that) of preserving for
future readers the books in his care, (and) to be at the
centre of the organic community which is the library, caring
not merely for his books but for the needs of every member
of the community, and for the chain of recorded tradition
which day-by-day is being handled, corrected, remoulded,
strengthened, added to and passed onward' (7). This conception
of a library may come as something of a culture shock to
those library school products where the study of historical
bibliography is anathema and where courses on mass communication, the literature of the working classes and various other
exercises in anti-intellectualism take place. The swinging
'sixties, *inter alia,* derided and devalued standards during
a period of rapid growth, and its legacy is not particularly
helpful in times of constraint. I would suggest that many
professional librarians would find it embarrassing to defend
the idea of a library in terms of Irwin's philosophy.

   Certainly, against a background of undergraduate demand
for its basic bread and butter, that is, the study place and
textbooks, scholarship and research are firmly put into place
save in those universities where the teaching of undergraduates
is the price to be paid for carrying out the real functions
of the institution. It is most important to realise here the
significant role played by the library in seating students,
and the stresses which can be thrown up elsewhere in the
institution by a severe curtailment of library opening hours.

   The extent to which teachers in higher education depend
upon the library for their teaching materials has not been
truly appreciated in times of growth, when almost everything
asked for has been provided. It is not peculiar that
librarians are now called upon to defend the need for
teachers' access to books and periodicals, rather than the
teachers themselves being accountable. The Librarian often
finds himself arguing the library case to those who would
deny him or her the resources and, then wearing another hat,
criticise the Librarian for failing to deliver the goods.

'In times of retrenchment'. Let us consider the word 'times'. Does it mean one period of time, i.e. now, or to use a more fashionable term, 'at this moment in time', or alternatively does it mean recurring periods of time?

Assuming that it is meant to represent a consecutive period, then it is pertinent to examine the timescale involved. On the 1st July 1981, Salford University learnt what grant the University Grants Committee aimed to give it for the two years 1982-84 (8). I would suggest that for most librarians employed in the university sector, the bad times start from that point. Yet in December 1975, subsequent to a tour of British university libraries, Harrison Bryan of the University of Sydney was writing that the end of the academic year 1974/75 found many British university libraries shivering in the cold wind of austerity and obsessed with the chill promise of more to come (9). Do those who remember the hiccup in library expansion regard that period as one where management became a challenge or merely tedious? Is there a comparison between the events of 1975 and, for example, the proposed 44% cut in grant to be inflicted on Salford? In the first twelve months subsequent to the 1981 UGC announcement about 100 of the Salford staff have volunteered to retire early, amongst them being the University Librarian. Another 300-350 will have to choose to leave in the next year or two if compulsory redundancy is to be avoided. In a paper given in March 1981 to the Library Association North Western Branch (10), I reminded members that libraries which had grown commensurately with their parent institutions cannot expect to escape unscathed when those institutions contract. This hard lesson has already been driven home in a number of institutions.

I do not regard that steady erosion of book purchasing power through inflation, which has been with us during the last decade, as retrenchment. Those who believed that an endless steady climb in bookfund was the natural order have been guilty of self delusion. This erosion was observed amongst academic libraries in the United States by Magrill and East some years ago (11) and accepted as inevitable.

The real cuts in the non-university or public sector of higher education appear to start from 1979. Polytechnics date from 1970; Colleges of Higher Education have an even shorter history. The poor level of resourcing which existed amongst those colleges translated into Polytechnics and

Colleges of Higher Education demanded substantial injection
of funds to fulfil the government of the day's promise that
both sides of the binary line were to be different but equal.
Certainly, libraries benefited from their obviousness which,
combined with pressure from students, teaching staff and the
Council for National Academic Awards, resulted in Polytechnic
libraries enjoying, for the most part, new building programmes
with substantial expansion in bookstock, periodical holdings
and staffing. In a few cases, largely because of local ignor-
ance and prejudice, library development has not been as
dramatic.

It is important to remember that the non-university
sector is financed by an entirely different method to that
obtaining in the universities. Manchester City Council, not
untypically, contributed from the rates to the AFE sector of
its Polytechnic until 1981. Although no longer financing the
Polytechnic except through its contribution for non-advanced
work, the local authority, as the channel through which the
Polytechnic is funded, can if it wishes divert 'Pool' money,
rightly intended for the Polytechnic, to other institutions
of Higher Education under its control, or even to other parts
of the education system should it so wish. Although
Manchester's additional support to Advanced Further Education
Pool money is no longer available, at least it has not pro-
gressed further in disadvantaging its Polytechnic by diverting
funds, although this dangerous practice is reported to have
begun elsewhere (12). The non-university sector therefore is
exposed to both national and local forces, and as there is
some evidence that libraries are carrying the brunt of the
cuts (13), then Polytechnic libraries can be doubly disadvantaged.
As an example of this, due to a 'New York type' local government financial crisis during the financial year 1980/81,
Manchester Polytechnic was required to return £1 million to
the City Exchequer in August, with the Polytechnic Library's
share being £100,000 from the remaining part of the bookfund
and the introduction of the frozen post mechanism. Similar
situations occurred in 1981/82 with two demands on the
Polytechnic for the return of £285,000 and £241,000 success-
ively, and on 5th July I was informed of a similar call
likely to occur during the current financial year.

These instances show a new trend in local authority
financial control, where planning appears to be non-existent
or where spending is subject to violent change according to
political whim. Institutions have no option but to respond,

and the response is likely to have an immediate effect on
the library.

Those who administer libraries have, for the most part,
administered in a climate of continuously increasing
resources, until very recently. I have sought today to
demonstrate that real cuts are a recent phenomenon and that,
prior to this, libraries have enjoyed 25 years of more or
less sustained growth. We have administered libraries in the
knowledge that certain extra resource input on an annual
basis has enabled us to avoid making unpleasant decisions,
to compromise where possible, to please over-demanding
lecturers and, in certain instances, to appease militant or
difficult members of library staff.

Dr. Ratcliffe, Librarian of the University of Cambridge,
told a gathering of senior librarians in Manchester two years
ago that any fool can manage a library in the good times. In
a Presidential Address to the LA North Western Branch last
year (14), I forecast that the next five years will sort the
men out from the boys, the women from the girls.

At a time when management needs maximum flexibility to
respond to rapidly changing situations, a spider's web of
constraints has been woven from threads of employment
protection legislation, restrictive practices, local government decisions and internal administrative decisions. For
example, in the financial year 1980/81 there was a suggestion
that Manchester Polytechnic could find a substantial proportion
of its imposed cuts by delaying maintenance work until the
following year. This decision was unacceptable because the
consequence would have been to deny another department funds
from which it in turn could offer up savings. Similarly, a
suggestion that a substantial Polytechnic building near the
city centre be abandoned in order to bring about savings was
considered impracticable because it was felt that the City
Council would not accept the substantial reduction in rate
revenue which would have been the case had the project gone
ahead. Typical also has been the unavoidable requirement for
reductions in staffing set against a no compulsory redundancy
policy.

How then does management respond to rapidly developing
or totally unforeseen circumstances which have a direct or
indirect effect upon the academic library?  To take the view,
as was proposed at the 1977 National Book League Conference (15),

that we should not try to cope with cuts but instead
concentrate on getting the cuts restored, is naive beyond
belief, suggesting that the academic library operates in a
vacuum. It gives positive support to the belief held in
certain quarters that libraries are there for the benefit
of librarians.

The first, and most important, principle to hammer home
to library staff is that the library is a part of its parent
institution, a sub-system within a system and not a free-
standing system in its own right. In former times, it is
probable that the library was not greatly affected by external
forces save funding, insofar as day-to-day administration
was concerned. Now, and in the foreseeable future, the library
is, and will be, more reactive to institutional decisions.

Let us consider the library as a sub-system and take as
an example the effect of the withdrawal of one-third of the
total bookfund half way through the financial year, as was
the case at Manchester Polytechnic in September 1980. In
reality this meant that practically all the remaining monograph fund disappeared, what was left after the raid being
less than necessary for renewal of periodicals payable in
December.

From past experience, it is known that pressure exerted
upon one part of the system invariably results in weaknesses
occurring elsewhere. In this instance it was likely that the
denial of new monograph purchase to teaching staff and students
would result in a considerable upsurge in inter-library loan
applications, so that a clamp-down in this area of library
activity was immediately necessary unless the savings were to
be jeopardised. From a position of unrestricted application,
therefore, by September 1980 the library had imposed a ban
on student applications save those countersigned by a member
of the teaching staff, and was limiting academic staff
applications to six per person per week. In that year 1980/81,
interlibrary loan applications fell by one-third of the
previous years total. Allowing for growth, the real drop was
of the order of 50%.

Considering the Polytechnic as a whole as a system, then,
the proposed cut of £100,000 from the bookfund in the mid-year
of 1980-81 was not simply a matter for sustained and loud
library opposition. In addition to responsibility towards the

library service, library staff have a corporate responsibility. The alternatives to bookfund cut were few and there is no doubt that if bookfund had been sustained then further cuts in non-teaching staff would have occurred, both within and without the library. It is worth bearing in mind here that without porters, access to buildings can be denied, and it is not generally appreciated to what extent academic libraries and their staffs are dependent upon others in order to flourish. Where cuts in cleaning services, telephones and heating, for example, have to be made across the board, the library must insist on fair treatment and not insist that it is a special case in these respects.

To what extent can research help management in these situations?  From what has already been said it should be apparent that the library has to react quickly to those situations which are now becoming all too familiar. Research implies a time scale and time is a commodity not generally available when fast decisions have to be made.

Much is made by library school educators and others of the need for adequate management information on which to base decisions. Indeed many speculate on the paucity of management information generally available. The reason for this is quite straightforward. The acquisition of management information on a continuous basis is generally expensive, although it is known that the computerisation of circulation systems reduces the cost of some information gathering. Nevertheless, those librarians who have not been fortunate enough to have a staffing base large enough to allow for permanent research assistants have chosen in the main to employ those who can be seen to be productive, i.e. date stampers, etc., rather than those whose research efforts are sometimes received with scepticism. One-off research projects, the large variety sometimes drawing British Library grants, often produce interesting results but which often have little value once a short period of time has elapsed.

Manchester Polytechnic Library has not had the benefit of research staff and yet has managed to mount some research projects in conjunction with the Department of Library and Information Studies at the same institution. An example of a one-off project of interest is provided by the study of the use of current periodical issues which was carried out some years ago in Manchester Polytechnic Library. Certainly, if this study had been undertaken in 1980 then the deletion of periodical titles in Law, the Humanities and Business Studies could have been carried out with less bloodshed than was the case. In the ideal library situation the monitoring of the use of current periodical titles should be an on-going activity. In Manchester Polytechnic Library it is estimated that the cost of this exercise would equal at least one half of one full-time assistant in view of the number of periodicals involved. In passing, it is interesting to note that the subject librarians of Manchester Polytechnic were able to use the photocopying declaration form as evidence of use of journal titles in the 1980 cancellation exercise.

I wish to make it clear that I am not anti-research. I am currently engaged on research into the origins of 20th century wood engraved illustration for a doctoral degree and I fully understand what is required by research in this connotation. The question I ask is whether or not the kind of activities which would provide the necessary information upon which to make correct decisions in times of stress can be defined as research. Is there such a thing as management research, and if so how do you define it? Much harm has been done to the cause of research by projects which have been devised and implemented at public expense either without proper planning or by a deliberate attempt to research an issue where it can be forecast that no conclusive evidence will result. I do not believe that the British Library's policy of putting money into research projects whilst having an aversion towards developmental projects has contributed to the good of British librarianship. I understand, for example, that subsequent to the publication and adoption of the Atkinson report, a substantial project has been mounted into the mechanical relegation of library materials based upon issue statistics. As the Librarian of an academic institution I believe that the use of library materials within the library is probably as great as the use of library materials issued for domestic consumption. I would put as much faith in relegating materials by measuring the thickness of the dust upon the top edge as in relegating materials by issue statistics alone.

It is a sad fact that many of my Polytechnic Librarian colleagues who have resigned, retired or died have been amongst the least pragmatic of us. Those with a fine eye and careful attention to detail, and who have presented immaculate documentation based upon careful research, have

found to their sorrow that vehemence and rhetoric have often
won the battle against reason in academic debate. Dispassionate
evaluation of the facts is foreign to those involved in
academic politics. Should this seem too cynical a view let
me say that I do consider management information to be
important, but more important still is the awareness of when
to impart management information and how much information
should be divulged on each occasion.

At a recent Examination Board which I attended an external
examiner pointed out that one of the troubles with teaching
sociology as a subject in a librarianship course was that no
decent sociological research had been undertaken with
reference to libraries. This reinforces the view of mine
that library research often avoids the fundamental questions
and concentrates on byways of library practice which are
comparatively unimportant. Perhaps this is a common British
trait which is related to fundamental decision-making in
management. As summed up by Peter Drucker (16) the importance
of decision-making in management is generally recognised, but
a good deal of the discussion tends to centre on problem-
solving, that is, on giving answers, and that is the wrong
focus. Indeed, the most common source of mistakes in management
decisions is the emphasis on finding the right answer rather
than the right question.

Ideally, the information which I should like to have, as
a matter of course and continuously updated, in order to plan
ahead, on which to base arguments for resources and to be
enabled to make the most effective use of those resources,
relates mainly to academic development, i.e., the way the
Polytechnic responds in relation to national and local policy.

First, an awareness of Government economic and educational
thinking is an essential requisite. That the two aspects are
related has been underlined forcibly in the public sector of
higher education by the recent but already infamous DES
circular (17) concerning the criteria for the approval of
new courses, stressing particularly the emphasis on national
technological need.

Next, an awareness of the collective views and likely
behaviour of the National Advisory Body would be helpful,
particularly as this organisation is likely to have considerable effect upon the continuance of existing Polytechnic
courses. As with the Council for National Academic Awards, it

is anticipated that this body will generate extensive and useful documentation.

A knowledge of regional and local patterns of development in educational organisation both at tertiary and secondary level is essential because of likely impact upon the institution. Some Polytechnic Librarians have experienced two mergers, and it is by no means certain that reorganisation of higher education has ceased. Useful information on other local situations is made available to its members by the Council of Polytechnic Librarians, which keeps in touch with developments within the Council of Local Education Authorities, as well as collecting and disseminating useful data, including comparative statistics. Library Association policy and developments within local public library authorities can affect staffing, and therefore have to be watched.

Much of this may seem irrelevant to librarians working at the coalface. It is however, a description of the needs of a director of a Polytechnic Library. Information on patterns of book use and user requirements, developments in information retrieval and in non-book media are examples of research for those who work in libraries. The Chief Librarian's role, as viewed by many professionals, is to obtain the money in order that 'they' can run the library.

With regard to the role of research in relation to the library manager, I would forecast that in the future he or she will be required to present more cogent arguments in the quest for resources. These arguments will have to be supported by data on a scale not hitherto required. Whether or not this supporting evidence, expensively acquired, gets more than a cursory glance I very much doubt.

Should the drought in academic library provision continue for a substantial period, I fear that matters will be improved only with a reawakening of student militancy. Those of my colleagues who remember past experiences will look forward to this with a heavy heart.

REFERENCES

1.   ROGERSON, I. Resource management in scarcity - staffing. *UC+R Newsletter*, 4, 1981, 8-10; *COPOL Newsletter*, 27, 1981, 11-14.

2.  GOODMAN, Lord. *In: Coping with cuts: a conference to examine the problems facing academic libraries in the late 1970's* (held at Holborn Library, Wednesday 13th July 1977). London: National Book League.

3.  KEMP, M. Letter to *The Guardian,* 21 June 1982.

4.  HOOK, J. Letter to *The Guardian,* 25 June 1982.

5.  IRWIN, R. *The heritage of the English library.* London: Allen and Unwin, 1964, pp.26-31.

6.  *ibid.* p.40.

7.  *ibid.* p.41.

8.  JONES, G. Salford: one year after the unkindest cut. *New Scientist,* 1 July 1982, 18.

9.  BRYAN, H. *University libraries in Britain.* London: Bingley, 1976, p.10.

10. ROGERSON, I. *Libraries in the next five years.* Paper delivered to the Library Association North West Branch, 4 March 1981.

11. MAGRILL, R.M. and EAST, M. Collection development in large university libraries. *In:* Harris, M.H. *(ed.) Advances in librarianship;* vol. 8. New York: Academic Press, 1978, pp.9-10.

12. Fight for pool rights begins. *The Times Higher Education Supplement,* 500, 4 June 1982, 1.

13. WALLIS, M. Coping with the cuts. *UC+R Newsletter,* 2, 1980, 2-3.

14. ROGERSON, I. *Libraries in the next five years. op.cit.*

15. GOFF, M. *In: Coping with cuts: a conference to examine the problems facing academic libraries in the late 1970's* (held at Holborn Library, Wednesday 13th July 1977). London: National Book League.

16.  DRUCKER, P. *The practice of management*. London;
     Heinemann, 1955, p.345.

17.  DEPARTMENT OF EDUCATION AND SCIENCE. *Approval of
     advanced further education courses in England*. DES
     circular No 1/82. London: Department of Education
     and Science, 9 February 1982.

DISCUSSION

1. Most of the discussion focussed upon the financial aspects of library management. One of the main concerns was the unpredictability of funding, especially since funds already allocated may be claimed back by the administration. Since funds were, therefore, at risk, there was some doubt that phasing of library expenditure, rather than spending an entire allocation immediately, was wise. Nevertheless, it was felt that planning ensures more effective expenditure.

2. There was some discussion of whether the library should claim special status, and special treatment, in relation to expenditure cuts. The speaker insisted that libraries should take their share of cuts, along with other departments or services.

3. It was thought that the fate of libraries, and the quality of library services, was more affected by extraneous factors such as the Council for National Academic Awards, student militancy, etc., than by library management.

4. It was thought that much library research is only useful if it is ongoing, to provide comparative data over time. This is expensive. It was also thought that research may often not be cost-effective; the cost of a project, for example, to identify periodical titles to be cancelled, may cost more than the amount of funds to be saved.

# THE FUTURE : IMAGES AND PROSPECTS

James Thompson

*Librarian, University of Reading*

I mean to talk about the effects of retrenchment in a wider context than merely that of the philosophy and aims of academic libraries, but certainly I must start on home territory. Anybody here today could rise to his or her feet and, entirely uninvited and unprepared, could expound at some bitter length about its effects in his or her library. It happens to be my privilege this morning; and I have got to say straightaway that it is important not to get too abstract about the effects.

At its meeting at the University of East Anglia in March of this year, the Standing Conference of National and University Libraries (SCONUL) received a detailed survey of the funding cuts in 1981-82. Here I would remind you that 1981-82 is only the first of three Sessions - 1981-82, 1982-83, 1983-84 - of what the Government has described as the restructuring of our universities; and I should further remind you that in each of these successive Sessions the reduction in funding is meant to get progressively worse.

SCONUL's survey of 1981-82 is bad enough to be going on with. One section of the survey, which I shall refer to immediately, relates to the effects of the cuts on services: automation, hours of opening, interlending, information services. Let me read out a substantial selection of the responses of the 56 libraries which replied to SCONUL's survey:

- Hours: reduced in term by 1 hour Monday - Thursday, by 5 hours on Friday, over all 6 service points. Interlending: budget ceiling of 15,000 interloans.

- Interlibrary loans cut from £16,000 to £10,000; information services fund from £6,250 to £3,400.

- Interlending cut from 2,250 to 1,750.

- Inter-library loan ceiling reduced from 12,000 to 9,700 p.a. No allocation for computer-based literature searching.

- Inter-library loans staff reduced by 25%. Reduction in opening hours one day per week.

- No funds available for continuation of automation developments. Inter-lending charges doubled.

- Inter-lending rationed.

- Opening hours cut because of staff losses. Automation plans affected by cuts in Computer Unit.

- Reduced inter-lending.

- Automation: developments from circulation to other housekeeping routines delayed. Opening hours: currently closing one hour earlier - may be further reductions as staff leave and are not replaced. Interlending: expected to achieve a 20% reduction in demand.

- Hours in outlying libraries cut due to staff losses. Automation plans delayed.

- The Library has 11 manned reading rooms: there has been a reduction of 680 opening hours in the year. Inter-lending: the amount available this year has been reduced by 57%.

- Supervised Xeroxing service hours reduced by 50% to cover staff losses.

- Closing at 6 pm, 4 nights weekly except in exam periods. Charging 50p per ILL (demand at present 40% of last year). Increased charges for IR (demand 30% of last year).

- Opening hours reduced as staff numbers dwindle.

- System closed at 5 pm every Friday. Two branches closed 5 pm every day. One branch closed most mornings. Main library partially closed for illness and no cover.

- Automation - no catalogue input in August and December.
- Closure on Sunday afternoons.
- 8 hours cut from weekend opening.

These examples, I trust, are sufficient to make my point about not getting too abstract.

I must go on to say that there is no credible philosophy of librarianship known to me which is served by reduction of opening hours. Neither are there any positive contemporary aims of librarianship which will be helped by a decreased inter-lending facility.

The thing to remember, the thing to keep in the forefront of one's mind, is that the present retrenchment is the result of external political and economic pressure. It is not the result of some fundamental re-thinking of educational philosophy as such, nor of a profound professional re-assessment on the part of librarians. The thrust is political: our Government's concept of a 'restructured' higher education system - slimmer, fitter, more finely tuned to the needs of our society, more accountable to our society in terms of material resources.

Whether or not anybody considers this political concept valid is no concern of ours today. As librarians working in academic libraries we have so far seen it only as an ill wind. Whether or not it might in the end do some incidental good, from the viewpoint of professional aims and philosophy, is I suppose the question to which we have been asked to address ourselves. To put it more bluntly: are there any long-term lessons to be learned from present short-term disasters? I say short-term disasters, not because I have some knowledge, possessed by nobody else, that the recession will be short-lived, but because no matter how meagre the resources made available to us are, we must achieve managerially a stable situation - even if a reduced one.

So I propose now to examine some specific effects of retrenchment on academic libraries, and I think I should start with staffing. In distant days, the rule of thumb was that a library spent 50% of its budget on staff, and 50% on library materials - books, journal subscriptions, binding, sundries. In the '60s and '70s this of course changed: the staff element crept up to 60%, the materials budget dropped to 40%. In some libraries the balance has reached 65%, 35%. It is not unusual to see a more pronounced version of this comparatively new kind of balance in North American libraries. In the annual report of one Canadian university library which came my way recently, the staff element of the budget was 68.4%, and can be explained, I think, as a derivative of sheer size of organisation.

However, it is the British context which concerns us today. The growing staff element of our budgets does not, unfortunately, necessarily mean more bodies providing desirable library services. In many of our libraries it means a very high proportion of very well-paid individual bodies: a kind of rash of professionals.

I would accept the charge that I have a bee in my bonnet on this subject. As long ago as 1974 (1) I argued that what so often passed professionally as being librarianship was nothing of the sort: that the only true tasks related to the selection of material; the organisation of material for use; reference services; and user instruction (by which I meant the interface with users at every level, formal and informal, individual and corporate). I dismissed as sub-professional such holy cows as book ordering, periodicals accessioning, preparing material for use, shelving and shelving arrangements, stocktaking, circulation control, and even cataloguing at bread-and-butter level. Other tasks again - such as accounting, maintaining buildings, personnel records, timetabling - I argued had nothing at all to do with professional librarianship as such. My general drift - and I do not wish to open up old wounds - was that in any given library staffing structure, the number of fully-fledged professionally-qualified graduates required was much smaller than traditionally and historically asserted.

One outcome of the current retrenchment has been an overdue endorsement of this view. Turning to the SCONUL survey, the picture which emerges is that though cuts have had to be made in staffing, in the short-term the only room for such manoeuvre lay in non-academic staff. Thus amongst the returns made to SCONUL are libraries reporting the loss of as many as 8 or 9 junior and clerical posts, with only five libraries maintaining staff numbers in those grades. In contrast, on the academic/professional side, where first there is less mobility anyway and second there is usually tenure, staff

reductions have been significantly smaller. The end result
is that our South American army of too many generals and
too few privates - or, if you like, our system of too many
Chiefs and too few Red Indians - has been aggravated to the
extent that our staffing structures are now nakedly, as
opposed to covertly, unbalanced. You ask any university
librarian or deputy librarian now which they would rather
have: an Assistant Librarian or two Library Assistants - or
even *one* Library Assistant - and the answer is of course the
latter.

This present situation ought to, and probably will, guide
any future recruitment philosophies. As I said earlier, I
have long believed our staff structures to be erroneous: the
next generation of libraries might begin to get it right.
Another force at work here, of course, is automation - the
de-skilling effects of which have been sufficiently examined
by commentators such as A.J. Meadows (2) and F.W. Lancaster
(3): and indeed, these effects are already very apparent in
libraries which have, for example, joined automation
co-operatives.

I do not know how many of you read *The Times*, but last
month, on June 10th, that newspaper carried a leader with
the title *Research in a cold climate*. In the middle of the
leader, in parentheses, was the following comment:


'Between 1972 and 1979 salaries and wages in university
libraries increased by 30 per cent in constant prices;
expenditure on books by only 11 per cent; while that
on periodicals actually fell by 1.5 per cent - in
spite of a publishing explosion and the commonly voiced
difficulties of keeping abreast of foreign journals.
One has no wish to libel the class of librarians, but
someone seems to have been looking after them better
than they have been looking after their libraries in
the 1970s.' (4).

Maybe that comment was unfair, but it does two things: one,
it rather bears out that our clients take my view of library
staffing, and two, it leads me neatly into consideration of
another area affected by retrenchment: what you might call,
or at least what I would call, the myth of the exploding
library.

For many years now, the vandals in our profession have
been putting about the idea that librarians, especially
academic librarians, have been pursuing megalomanic policies
of library growth, have been trying to build an Alexandrian
Library on every campus. This may possibly be true of our
more affluent American cousins - in the University of
Pittsburgh, maybe, where Professor Allen Kent's research (5)
has demonstrated that 40 per cent of its library collections
have never been used - but as far as the United Kingdom is
concerned, well, chance would be a fine thing. In truth, for
about the last ten years, we have been financially incapable
of maintaining an adequate level of periodicals provision,
and have become increasingly more selective and restrictive
in the matter of book purchase.

Turning once again to the SCONUL survey of 1981-82, a
quick check produces the following selection of individual
reports:

- £9,000 worth of periodicals cancelled.
- Books - reduced from £120,000 to £53,000. Periodicals
  - subscriptions cut by £16,500.
- Periodicals cut by 10%. Expenditure on books cut by 30%.
- Acquisitions and binding minus £100,000 overall.
- Book allocation down by c.23% from last year. Plans
  for serials cancellations.
- 29% cut in expenditure on books.
- £150,000 cut.

Admittedly these examples are amongst the worst: but the
picture overall is ominously overcast. It does rather put
paid to the Atkinsonian myth of bibliographical flab:
politically at any rate, though in reality - if you would
care to read the chapters by Dr F.W. Ratcliffe (6) and
Norman Roberts (7) in the book I edited on university library
history - it always was a myth.

In relation to library collections, the particular problem
which retrenchment points up is: now what do we do?  If we
accept the current professional philosophy of having an
'access' policy, as opposed to a 'holdings' policy, who is
going to be able to afford the 'holdings' to which everybody

else is going to have to turn to for 'access'? Somebody has to fulfil this function, but who? I shall return to this question at the end of my paper, when I come to examine the wider aspects of retrenchment.

As a trailer though, I could observe that a number of us sometimes are tempted to think that university libraries have become too important to be left to the whims of individual universities. And as an aside, is it not rather ironic that on one hand our profession is promulgating the entirely proper and sensible notion of 'access', while at grassroots level a British Library Lending Division form is now £1.75, and most libraries known to you and me have had to place considerable and unprecedented restrictions on inter-library loan facilities?  Now you could take this two ways: individual libraries could backtrack to a more positive holdings policy, though where the money, the staff and the buildings would come from is unknowable; or, more practically, you could say that the time has come for us once again to re-examine our whole inter-library loan structure. Are the services of the monolith at Boston Spa, our mainstay and lifeline since the '60s, eventually going to be priced beyond our means?  Are there any possibilities of a more economic alternative: either technologically (such as some really notable advance in facsimile transmission), or organisationally, or by rejigging the system on a different basis altogether (for example, exploiting the growing databases of regional cooperatives)?

Inter-library loan facilities are of course only one of the many library services which have taken a knock as the result of retrenchment. I suppose we may have learned that we have been a little wasteful of expensive inter-loan facilities; practically everybody cites the apocryphal foreign postgraduate student ordering 100 journal articles just because some of the titles sounded as if they might be relevant. But apart from a necessary and enforced tightening up of procedures, such as requiring that same student to obtain his supervisor's signature on all of his requests, I do not think any of us have concluded that inter-library loans can ever be regarded as an optional extra.

As for other services, all of us regret any diminution in hours of opening. I do not think there can be any valid argument that long opening hours are a bad thing: our quite proper defensive stance has always been that a library represents a substantial, cumulatively appreciating, investment on the part of our university or polytechnic institution, and it would be a waste of that investment to reduce access to it. When a library is closed, its collections are valueless. I suppose the best we can do in a period of retrenchment is to keep the place open for as long hours as possible, but perhaps to have long patches of minimal service. Even then I am not too sure of the wisdom of that course of action, because whatever time a user chooses to come into a library, he or she is not really served if the place seems like the Marie Celeste.

Other services: well, there is photocopying. In an odd way, all of us often seem to deprecate this service to some extent, while at the same time providing it in increasing measure. I think though we should keep in mind the high value our users place on it. In my more basic moments, I sometimes think that all that the majority of our clients - that is, the students - require of us is a large hall, multiple copies of undergraduate texts, and a great battery of photocopiers, and that having this they would be quite satisfied. So one could argue that though supervised photocopying services could be sacrificed in times of retrenchment, the coin-ops must stay. That is, of course, the law of copyright permitting, and continuing to permit. If changes in copyright were to require supervision of photocopying, I think we would have a real problem on our hands.

An inter-library loans service, adequate hours of opening, photocopying facilities: those are basic provisions, and by various stratagems we shall probably manage to keep them going. But there is another level of service, not so obviously basic, which is suffering as a result of retrenchment. This is reference service, and linked with that, user instruction. To start with the latter: user instruction has collected its fair share of odium, mainly on the basis of the argument that if, for example, a customer cannot find what he wants on the shelves of his supermarket, what the supermarket manager does is not organise courses in supermarket use, but instead re-organises his supermarket so that people *can* find what they want. In libraries, however, it is not just that our systems are daft - out-dated classification schemes, unusable catalogues, and so on - but that, in very large libraries at any rate, they are too historically and expensively entrenched for short-term revision; so the poor user *has* to have some guidance. In a library in times of retrenchment,

the user is lucky to find any staff member free to help,
let alone teach him to get the best out of what the library
has to offer.

In terms of reference help, the present situation is
particularly hard. It may be as a result of my own personal
history as a librarian, but I have always considered
reference work to be librarianship at its very best, at its
most expert, at its most rewarding, at its most appreciated.
Currently our staffs are so busy hewing wood and drawing
water that they have to skimp on reference work. I consider
that a tragedy. Its most acute contemporary manifestation
is that an increasing number of libraries, with facilities
for on-line retrieval, cannot find staff-time to provide
more than one or two searches a week.

This leads me straight into a very worrying aspect of
retrenchment. You will recall the theory behind today's
economic policies: the vision of a restructured future,
leaner, fitter, more muscular, more attuned to society's
needs. In terms of library and information services, the
*professional* equivalent of this vision, and one, if I may
say so, more realistically based, is of the electronic
library.

Very few of you here need a separate lecture from me on
the possibilities. You know already of the millions of
surrogate references in on-line databases such as DIALOG.
You know equally well of the bibliographic databases - OCLC,
MARC, REMARC. You know of full-text systems, such as LEXIS,
in the field of law. You have heard of videotex systems, of
which Prestel is the outstanding example. You have heard
of the possibilities of facsimile transmission, of storage
on video discs, of the prospect sooner or later of electronic
publishing. You have seen some of the fruits of OCR techniques,
and many of you will be using word processors and microcomputers.

I am deliberately compacting a whole range of developments,
but the umbrella for all of them is the potent combination of
computer and telecommunications: 'telematics'. For all of us
here to stay in the business of storing, retrieving and
exploiting information, we will have to remain heavily
involved in these new ventures. And that costs money which in
a time of retrenchment we do not have.

So far we have made considerable efforts to keep involved.
On-line services, videotex facilities, machine-readable
catalogues: we have them already. But keeping pace with such
ventures might, in financial terms, soon begin to slip out
of our grasp. If that did happen, in terms of professional
aims and objectives, we would be sunk.

You will recall that even in the 1981-82 SCONUL survey,
there were some warning signs: 'No allocation for computer-
based literature searching' - 'No funds available for
continuation of automation developments' - 'Automation plans
affected by cuts in Computer Unit' - 'Automation plans
delayed'. Curiously though, there has been a brighter side.
Though recurrent moneys have been under pressure, funds for
equipment and furniture seem relatively easier, at least
in the university sector. The outlay on systems such as GEAC
is not small, but some university libraries have managed it.
To a lesser extent, this is where our increased range of
hardware has originated. The philosophy might be formulated
in the form: if you cannot afford a person, buy a machine.
If you are feeling a little sanguine, it could perhaps be
argued that this is an instance where, maybe, the ill wind
has blown good.

But being able to buy the hardware does not of course
crack the problem. The basic trouble is the capricious nature
of our funding. In the course of Session 1981-82, the UGC did
realise that the cuts might be falling heavily on libraries.
In February 1982 Dr Parkes, the Chairman, wrote to all
universities noting that library services are particularly
vulnerable because of the relative ease with which quick
changes can be made to planned expenditure on them, and
suggesting that part of the addition he was making to block
recurrent grants might be applied to them.

This perception on the part of the UGC was much appreciated
by university librarians: indeed, some university institutions
even took heed of it. In my view though, academic libraries
will forever remain at risk if they continue to be financed,
as they are at present, in isolation from one another, and
irrespective of any national library context. Here, I imagine,
I may be reverting to a theme begun by Norman Higham, at the
very outset of this conference. If the concluding part of my
paper, on the wider aspects of retrenchment, carries naturally
on from his opening address, I shall not be displeased to
create the impression that your whole weekend has been elegantly
structured.

I have commented elsewhere, in a paper I gave to a Library Association workshop last summer (8) that though academic libraries do of course service the research and undergraduate needs of their parent institutions, they go way beyond this in potential and capacity. I quoted then, and I shall now quote again, an American writer, Charles Osburn, who in 1979 published a study called *Academic research and library resources*. Osburn commented rather worriedly :

> 'There is reason to believe that large academic libraries have become inclined to behave quite independently of their actual constituencies, who may not always hold the same view of the purpose and value of the library that is held by those who manage the library collections.... Faculty and librarian perceptions about the value and role of collections may differ, since librarians have both professional and personal vested interests; however, library literature gives no evidence that the implications of these divergent perspectives have ever been of interest to the academic library profession, which is symptomatic of a closely guarded independence in university libraries, especially in the area of collection development.' (9)

Too true. Osburn, though, then goes on to say that this dichotomy of attitude does not bode well for large academic libraries 'in the difficult fiscal times that are foreseen for the remainder of the twentieth century.'

It so happens that my philosophy of librarianship runs totally counter to Osburn's, and I shall tell you why. It has always seemed to me inevitable that academic libraries, if they really flourished and grew, would evolve as organisations increasingly independent of their parent institutions. The obvious example which occurs to me is the Bodleian. I suppose the Bodleian could be regarded as the Library of the University of Oxford, but in truth of course it is as famous in its own right as its parent institution: it figures nationally as part of the United Kingdom library scene, and internationally it stands as one of the world's great libraries. To say, as Osburn is presumably saying, that the Bodleian should mend its ways and relate its activities more strictly to the academic needs of its constituents, is  patent nonsense. Ah, you may say, but the Bodleian is the Bodleian and is quite exceptional, and not at all like the middle-sized Library of

the University of X or the Polytechnic of Y. That is bound
to be true, in absolute terms - nowhere else is like the
Bodleian - but in the terms of my argument, I beg to differ.

If you look at the history of the growth of academic
libraries - I am not so knowledgeable on the history of
polytechnic and college libraries - the overall impression
one gets is that academic libraries have grown almost in
spite of, rather than because of, the attitude of their parent
institutions. Norman Roberts (10) for example has remarked
that over the years university libraries have been ungenerously
funded to a 'marked and consistent' degree. Where there has
been any effort to look after them, it has usually come from
outside - the outstanding example here is the 1967 Parry
Report, the University Grants Committee's Report of the
Committee on Libraries. A more recent example, though perhaps
of a rather perverse kind, was the Atkinson Report: but even
that, after all, was based on the premise that the well-being
of academic libraries is a crucial issue.

Then again, pitching all of this at another level
altogether, look around your own libraries, and what do you
see?  The biggest influences on their organisational development have come externally, from other *library* institutions
- not other *university* or *polytechnic* or *college* institutions.
For example, if we would now claim to be service-oriented,
this was not at the behest of our academic faculty, but
because we learned from the public library sector, and
because we imported the American standards of service which
had been set by pioneers such as Melvil Dewey.

Look at our buildings, at least at our recent buildings.
Left to themselves - as I have also said elsewhere - I
suspect our vice-chancellors and principals would always
have favoured the monumental approach to university library
buildings: the Gothic cathedral, the Renaissance palace,
the mini-Bodleian. Librarians, however, conscious of the
service functions required of present-day academic libraries,
have very successfully promoted flexible, adaptable, usable
structures. Equally, we have imported and imposed standard
cataloguing and classification systems; we operate cooperative
storage and acquisitions schemes; we join automation networks;
we see that our staffs are educated and trained to a national
standard.

In truth, and in reality, apart from receiving our funds
on a local basis, and operating locally within the procedural
framework of our parent institutions, by and large we are all
doing our own librarian thing: a kind of Militant Tendency
group within the academic world.

Moreover, our users take our view, and accept our
perceptions also. To a user, a library is a library is a
library, and he or she is suitably bemused to find three
successive blocks in a town devoted to what are called the
public library, the polytechnic library, and the university
library.

The Library Association pointed to this reality in its
recent *Statement on the university cuts* (11) (approved by
Council on 15 June 1982). The covering letter which
accompanied the statement commented that the present attacks
on university financing did damage far beyond the universities
themselves, a fact not apparently appreciated 'by those outside
of the profession' who are responsible for allocating resources.
The statement stresses the important role of academic libraries
'in the national pattern of information provision'; points out
that the overall reduction in acquisitions by academic
libraries has particular significance for the 'national stock'
of libraries; and that the curtailment of the services of
academic libraries - such as the reduction of evening and
weekend opening hours - discriminates in particular against
many types of 'outside reader' (for example, professional
groups, such as lawyers, social workers, public health
inspectors, architects).

The Library Association's statement also makes reference
to the second report of the Library and Information Services
Council, *The future development of libraries and information
services* (12) which quite properly places academic libraries
in the context of what it calls the 'national order'. Norman
Higham has already dwelt on the co-ordinating role not only
of LISC, but also of the Office of Arts and Libraries.
Similarly co-ordinative, and cohesive, is the work of the
Library Association itself, of the Standing Conference of
National and University Libraries, of the University, College
and Research Section of the Library Association, and of the
myriad co-operative groups which characterise our profession.

The philosophy which retrenchment has confirmed for me is
the broad one that all libraries are part of one structure.

Either we hang together, or we get hanged separately. In my opinion no library method or procedure, system or technique, makes much sense in isolation. Neither does collection building, nor collection reduction. Retrenchment has hardened my longstanding view on this.

May I say in conclusion that I think it marvellously fortunate that just when retrenchment has sunk its teeth into our vitals, that at the very same time a variety of other external pressures - spearheaded by the realisation that information is the world's most valuable commodity - have led to the political realisation that libraries and information services must be harnessed nationally. True, this does not offer much short-term hope that you and I will be able to re-open our libraries on Sunday afternoons, but in my view it certainly removes any serious prospect of *long-term* neglect.

REFERENCES

1.  THOMPSON, J. *Library power*. London: Bingley, 1974.

2.  MEADOWS, A.J. *New technology developments in the communication of research during the 1980s*. Leicester: Primary Communications Research Centre, 1980.

3.  LANCASTER, F.W. *Towards paperless information systems*. New York: Academic Press, 1978.

4.  *The Times*, 10 June 1982, p.13.

5.  KENT, A. *et al*. *Use of library materials: the University of Pittsburgh study*. New York: Marcel Dekker, 1979.

6.  RATCLIFFE, F.W. The growth of university library collections in the United Kingdom: *In:* Thompson, J. *(ed)*. *University library history*. London: Bingley, 1980, pp.5-32.

7.  ROBERTS, N. Financing of university libraries in the United Kingdom. *In:* Thompson, J. *(ed)*. *University library history*. London: Bingley, 1980, pp.109-127.

8.  THOMPSON, J. *Educational policy and academic library development*. Paper delivered at the Library Association International Summer Workshop, 1981.

9.  OSBURN, C. *Academic research and library resources: changing patterns in America*. Westport, Connecticut: Greenwood Press, 1979, p.131.

10. ROBERTS, N. *op.cit.*

11. LIBRARY ASSOCIATION. Statement on the university cuts. London: Library Association, April 1982. (LSC 571).

12. DEPARTMENT OF EDUCATION AND SCIENCE OFFICE OF ARTS AND LIBRARIES. *The future development of libraries and information services*. London: HMSO, 1982. (Library Information Series No.12).

DISCUSSION

Discussion centred upon the following issues:

1.  There was a feeling that it was common to have over-
    qualified people in lower grades doing simple tasks.
    Some people, for example cataloguers, are not re-
    deployable. The need is often for porters, typists,
    assistants to stamp out the books.

2.  Library schools are over-producing librarians. They
    should be concentrating on continuing education for
    those that already have jobs. It was agreed that the
    problem lay in the fact that library schools' staffing
    levels are determined by the numbers of full-time
    students.

3.  The management of libraries requires an awareness of
    the political context in which libraries and their
    parent institutions operate. Decisions are political,
    for example the creation of polytechnics, rather than
    the expansion of existing universities, which could
    easily have been adopted.

# LIST OF PARTICIPANTS

| | |
|---|---|
| R. ASPREY | British Library Lending Division |
| Jim BASKER | Portsmouth Polytechnic |
| John BATE | Napier College, Edinburgh |
| Sue BLOOMFIELD | Hatfield Polytechnic |
| Jovana BROWN | The Evergreen State College, Washington |
| Antonia BUNCH | Dept. of Librarianship, University of Strathclyde |
| Barbara BURTON | University of London |
| Fred CHAMBERS | Cambridgeshire College of Arts and Technology |
| Daphne CLARK | Hatfield Polytechnic |
| David CLOW | Dept. of Library Studies, Queens University, Belfast |
| Mary COOPER | Swansea University College |
| D WYN EVANS | University of Exeter |
| Keith FARMERY | University of Manchester |
| Geoffrey FORD | University of Southampton |
| Nigel FORD | Dept. of Information Studies, University of Sheffield |
| Maureen FORREST | Cairns Library, Oxford |
| Lesley GILDER | Centre for Library and Information Management, University of Loughborough |
| John HALL | School of Librarianship, Leeds Polytechnic |
| Michael HANNON | University of Liverpool |
| Colin HARRIS | Centre for Research on User Studies, University of Sheffield |
| Keith HARRIS | Newcastle upon Tyne Polytechnic |
| Michael HEINE | School of Librarianship and Information Studies, Newcastle upon Tyne Polytechnic |

| | |
|---|---|
| Norman HIGHAM | University of Bristol |
| Alan HOPKINSON | Trent Polytechnic |
| David HOUSE | Brighton Polytechnic |
| Sue HOWLEY | British Library Research and Development Dept. |
| Monica HUMPHRIES | King's College, University of London |
| Brian HUTCHIN | Derby Lonsdale College of Higher Education |
| Clare JENKINS | King's College, University of London |
| Ray LESTER | Graduate School of Business Studies, University of London |
| Brendan LOUGHRIDGE | Dept. of Information Studies, University of Sheffield |
| K. MERRY | British Library Lending Division |
| Bernard NAYLOR | University of Southampton |
| Judith PALMER | Cairns Library, Oxford |
| Mike PATTINSON | Hull College of Higher Education |
| Philip PAYNE | City of London Polytechnic |
| Stephen PEARSON | Hudsons Bookshops Ltd. |
| Andrew PHILIPS | British Library Reference Division |
| Warwick PRICE | Huddersfield Polytechnic |
| Stephen ROBERTS | Centre for Library and Information Management, University of Loughborough |
| Elizabeth RODGER | University of Sussex |
| Ian ROGERSON | Manchester Polytechnic |
| John RUSSELL | University of Salford |
| Alexandra SHAW | Goldsmiths' College, University of London |
| Malcolm SMITH | British Library Lending Division |
| Richard SMITH | Sheffield City Polytechnic |
| Peter STONE | University of Sussex |
| Peter TAYLOR | Aslib |
| James THOMPSON | University of Reading |